ROYAL FLUSH

The Black Coat Script Library

ROYAL FLUSH

screenplay by
Randy & Jean-Marc Lofficier

A Black Coat Press Book

Acknowledgements: We are indebted to Will Eisner for his gracious permission to appear in this script, Jay Stephens for the use of one of his characters on the cover and David McDonnell for proofreading the typescript.

Royal Flush screenplay © 1996 by Randy & Jean-Marc Lofficier.
Cover art Copyright © 2004 by Jay Stephens.

Visit our website at www.blackcoatpress.com

WILL EISNER STUDIOS, INC.

August 12, 1996,

Dear Jean-Marc,

Just had a chance during my recent vacation to read
Royal Flush.

I enjoyed it and it lived up to the promise held out by
your brief telling of it at dinner at San Diego.

I hope it gets picked up again... These things *do* happen,
you know.

Warm regards,

Will

Introduction

"Write about what you know," is one of the most often repeated clichés that aspiring writers are likely to receive. What we know is comics, and with *Royal Flush*, we decided to just do that. But while comics do play a vital role in the story, the structure and the wish-fulfillment aspects that lie at its core owe their existence to the works of the brilliant French playwright Marcel Pagnol, known in this country for the theatrical feature releases of *Jean de Florette* and *Manon of the Springs*.

Marcel Pagnol (1895-1974) was a playwright turned filmmaker who wrote and produced a series of life-affirming pictures that celebrated the glories of Provence. He had an unerring ear for dialogue and was a master at creating characters with deep, profound humanity. Of all his films, one of our favorites is *Le Schpountz* (1938) starring Fernandel in the role of Irénée Fabre, a naive but endearing young *provençal* who so desperately wants to become a great movie star that, against all odds, he succeeds–as a comic, however, not a dramatic actor as he initially intended.

Royal Flush is also about the triumph of the heart over all of the harsh realities of a cruel world. Like Irénée, Elliot just has no idea of what he is up against, but he eventually succeeds thanks to his innate goodness, resourcefulness and the help of his friends–always a crucial chorus in all of Pagnol's plays.

A detail worthy of note (at least to comic book readers) is that the reclusive comic book artist millionaire William Rensie is none other that our friend, the

7

equally legendary Will Eisner–who actually used that pseudonym to draw *Hawks from the Sea* in the 1940s–who, of course, is anything but mysterious. We owe a debt of gratitude to Will for having agreed to appear in this story. It was (is?) our dream for him to actually play the part in a cameo, should *Royal Flush* be made–and had we any say in it.[1]

Royal Flush was initially optioned for the late John Candy to star, but the comic's untimely death in 1994 put an end to that notion.

Randy & Jean-Marc Lofficier

---

[1] This was written before the sad loss of Will Eisner in January 2005. He was true and wonderful gentleman, who will be sorely missed by many. We were proud to call him our friend. (NDA)

ROYAL FLUSH

Royal Flush

FADE IN:

<u>EXT. SANTA BARBARA - DAY</u>
on a beautiful Saturday morning. The sky is very clear and bright blue. It's going to be a hot day, but the temperature is still pleasant.

The atmosphere of this medium-sized California coastal town is very peaceful, quiet, laid-back. A feeling of the 1960s still lingers in the air. The people are mellow. They don't care much for their big city neighbor, Los Angeles.

CAMERA PULLS IN on JESSE'S CAR, moving through the traffic.

It is a second-hand yellow Toyota, darting between the other cars like a firefly. It stands out among the large American cars that lumber along the tree-lined streets.

CLOSE-UP on JESSE
who is an attractive, athletic blonde woman in her late twenties or early thirties. She conveys spunk, and a sense of humor. She is wearing a pastel-colored outfit that looks stylish, but was probably purchased at Wal-Mart. She is the kind of woman who, once she makes an emotional commitment, will stick by it. She is intelligent, decisive, and her head is set squarely on her shoulders.

FAVOR JESSE'S CAR again as it approaches a small, outdoor shopping center. In a corner, squeezed between an Italian deli and a dry cleaning store, we SEE a small shop that looks like it has known better days.

CAMERA PULLS IN on the store. A hand-painted sign in the window identifies it as the "ROYAL FLUSH COMICS" shop.

EXT. ROYAL FLUSH COMICS - DAY
Jesse parks the car, gets out and walks towards the store.

INT. ROYAL FLUSH COMICS - DAY
The inside of the shop is filled with racks and racks of plastic-wrapped comic books, rows of shelves carrying cardboard boxes filled with comics filed in no apparent order, etc.

The air has a dusty quality to it. A few superhero posters adorn the walls, adding some color to the surroundings, but unsuccessfully hiding the places where the plaster has fallen.

SEVERAL KIDS in the b.g. are going through the racks, picking out the latest stuff and swapping superhero gossip.

CLIFF stands behind a glass display counter which is filled with rare comics and luxury reprint editions.

He is a very portly man, with a warm complexion. He is dressed in jeans, and wears a funny rabbit T-shirt that says "Captain Carrot Lives!" Because of his large size, Cliff relies heavily on his sense of humor to charm others. But, he is no buffoon. Behind his easy-going expression, his mind sees all the angles of a situation and can quickly calculate its potential for profit or loss. Cliff is very loyal to his friends, and will do anything to help them–up to a point.

He smiles as he adds up a customer's tab.

>   CLIFF
>   There. That'll be $320.
>   (he laughs)
>   No, I seem to have made a mistake. It's only
> $10.55.

THE CUSTOMER is obviously familiar with Cliff's favorite joke. He pulls his wallet out to pay.

>   CLIFF
>   Have you seen the latest "Wonder" books?
>   We only got a few this week. I put one aside
>   for you.

Cliff pulls a brightly-colored book from under the counter and hands it over to the Customer.

>   CLIFF
>   Beautiful stuff. Great story.

The Customer starts leafing through the pages.

ELLIOT suddenly appears from behind a row of boxes. He is a tall, lanky man in his mid-thirties, with dark, curly hair. In spite of his unshaven and rather unkempt appearance, he radiates charm. He is a very attractive, almost rakish, man. Like Cliff, he is dressed in jeans and a T-shirt.

He is a child of the 1960s. He skates through life, without having taken on the usual adult responsibilities. He has never had to hold down a nine to five job. Like his partner, Cliff, Elliot eats, breathes and sleeps comics. He is, however, more generous. He is the type of person that would let a customer get by without paying if he couldn't afford to.

> ELLIOT
> (excited)
> Hey, Cliff, you'll never guess what I just found!

Cliff leaves his customer and walks from behind the counter.

We SEE that Elliot is standing a few feet away from a desk, previously hidden by the shelves. The top of the desk is covered with 3x5 index cards, a few books and a huge stack of comic books.

Elliot shoves a comic book in front of Cliff.

> ELLIOT
> Guess what. Will Rensie was really the guy that drew all the "Protector" stories during the War!

> CLIFF
> (genuinely interested)
> Wow! That's why all the girls looked so gorgeous.

                    ELLIOT
Yeah... That's what made me suspicious in the
first place. Rensie was always real secretive
about his work. He never signed any of his stuff.
It makes his art awfully hard to track down!
                    (a beat)
He came in on "The Protector" when Sullivan
was drafted. He started to ink his stuff and
then...

Jesse suddenly enters the shop, interrupting Elliot's ex-
planations.

                    JESSE
Hi, honey! Hi, Cliff!
                    (to Cliff)
I've come to collect your partner for lunch.

Elliot looks at his watch, dumbstruck.

                    ELLIOT
My God! It's already 12:30! It can't be...

He looks at Jesse apologetically.

                    ELLIOT (cont'd)
You sure you can't have lunch alone, honey?
I've been trying to finish the chapter of my book
on the '40s, and I still have all the '50s comics
to index...

He points at the stack of comics.

                    JESSE
                   (upset)
This morning, you said that we'd have lunch
together. We never see each other anymore.
You're always at the shop...

                    ELLIOT
OK, OK! No problem. It's fine... I can finish
it later.

He walks back to his desk, puts the stack of comics away
on a shelf and grabs his jacket.

                    ELLIOT
                  (to Cliff)
If you need me, I'll be home all afternoon.

They leave the shop together.

Cliff then turns towards the Customer who, by now, has
almost read the entire book.

                    CLIFF
You like it?

                   CUSTOMER
Well, the art isn't very good...

Cliff raises an eyebrow.

                   CUSTOMER
                  (quickly)
...but I'll take it.

Cliff beams.

                    CLIFF
          That'll be another $7.95.

EXT. SANTA BARBARA - DAY
Jesse's car enters a modest looking, residential area.
Jesse is at the wheel.

INT. JESSE'S CAR - DAY
The atmosphere in the car is a bit tense. Jesse obviously
wants to say something, but hesitates. Finally, she starts.

                    JESSE
          Bennett asked me to do some overtime this
          afternoon.

                    ELLIOT
                (annoyed)
          What! But you just said that we didn't see each
          other...

                    JESSE
                (interrupting)
          I know! I know! But we need the money.
          Do you think it's easy for me? You know how
          much you brought home from the shop last
          week? You know how much groceries cost?
          And I only buy the necessities!

                    ELLIOT
          Business has been kind of slow lately.

JESSE

Business is *always* slow in that shop. Besides,
anything you do make, you spend on more
comics.

Elliot becomes agitated.

ELLIOT
(emotionally)
But I love comics!

JESSE

Well, *I* love nice clothes, but you don't see me
buying them all the time.

ELLIOT

It's not the same thing. Comics don't cost as
much as clothes. Anyway, Cliff gives me a
break.

A pause.

Jesse takes this opportunity to discuss something that has
been bothering her for some time.

JESSE

Ah! While we're on the subject of Cliff, if you
didn't invite him to dinner so often, things
would be easier.

ELLIOT

Honey, he's my best friend! Besides, he likes
you so much.

                    JESSE
        If you ask me, the only thing he likes is that
        fancy car of his.

Elliot rushes to defend his friend.

                    ELLIOT
        That's unfair! He doesn't have anyone to spend
        his money on.

                    JESSE
        Well, I'd like some fancy things too! Look at
        this dump we live in. I want a house of our own!

                    ELLIOT
                  (feeling guilty)
        I know, sweetheart. You know how much
        houses cost. We don't have the money for the
        downpayment. Just wait a little longer until I get
        my book published.

                    JESSE
        I'll believe that when I see it. You've been
        working at it for five years now.

                    ELLIOT
                  (hurt)
        I'm not goofing off! It takes a lot of work. This
        book is going to be the most comprehensive
        history of comics ever written. I want us both to
        be proud of it when it's done.

Jesse immediately regrets her jibe. She doesn't want to
make Elliot feel that he is not pulling his own weight.

Her remarks hit too close to home, and can hurt their relationship. Besides, she loves him and accepts him as he is.

> JESSE
> You're right, honey. I'm sorry. But meanwhile, we should be happy that I have my job at the bank.

Elliot doesn't hold a grudge. In his typical fashion, he has already put her remarks out of his mind.

> ELLIOT
> Well, your mother did warn you.
> (imitating Jesse's mother's voice)
> "You'll never get anywhere with that good-for-nothing bum..."

Jesse laughs at Elliot's impersonation. The ice is broken.

> JESSE
> Well, she was right, wasn't she?

> ELLIOT
> Just wait a little bit longer, honey. Someday, we'll have enough money to buy you a *biiiig* house! You'll never have to complain again about all the comics I leave laying around the apartment. We'll have a whole room just for comics!

Jesse gets caught up in Elliot's fantasy.

JESSE
I'd rather have a ranch...

ELLIOT
OK, then. A big ranch! With lots of horses!

EXT. SANTA BARBARA - DAY
The car turns into a small street that leads to

EXT. APARTMENT COMPLEX - DAY
The car pulls into the driveway of an apartment complex where a sign spells "RANCHO PARADIS-" (the "E" has fallen off and not been replaced). The building looks like it could use a fresh coat of paint.

Jesse pulls the car into its space.

INT. JESSE'S CAR - DAY
JESSE
(turning towards Elliot)
Well, pardner, will you help me carry the groceries?

EXT. APARTMENT COMPLEX - DAY
Elliot gets out of the car, goes to the trunk and takes out two brown paper bags. Sticking out of the tops, "plain-wrapped" packages are clearly visible.

Jesse walks up a rickety flight of outdoor steps. Elliot follows her.

They stop at the door of their apartment. She turns the key. The door sticks slightly, then opens. They enter.

INT. APARTMENT - DAY
The apartment is a small one. It consists of a living room/dining room combination, with a small kitchen area off to one side.

There are few furnishings, and the carpet is well worn. Stacks of comics lay around the floor, and on top of a tired-looking couch. The appliances in the kitchen have seen better days.

Elliot puts the groceries on the dining room table.

Jesse grabs an apron to protect her dress while she cooks.

> JESSE
> I'll fix lunch now. Why don't you straighten up a little bit in the meantime?

Elliot looks around and shrugs.

> ELLIOT
> I don't feel like it right now. I'll do it after you've gone.

In the kitchen, Jesse kind of sighs, then turns to the stove. She breaks two eggs into a frying pan.

JESSE'S POV - THE PAN
with the two eggs starting to fry.

> DISSOLVE TO:

The same pan, now dirty, sitting in a sinkful of water.

CAMERA PANS BACK, revealing other signs of Jesse and Elliot having finished their lunch. An hour or so has gone by.

Jesse is cleaning up the table. Elliot sits at the table, finishing a cup of coffee.

                    ELLIOT
          So, why do you have to go to work on a
          Saturday afternoon? I thought they had
          abolished slavery.

                    JESSE
          Bennett wants me to help him clean up the
          archives. Apparently, the Federal Examiners are
          coming next week. We haven't been audited in
          ages. There's stuff in there that goes back all the
          way to the 1890s, when they opened the Bank.

                    ELLIOT
          Really?

                    JESSE
          Yeah. They have to keep everything, you know.
          Federal regulations. We have some pretty old
          accounts...
                    (looking at her watch)
          Oh! I better be going or I'll be late!

Jesse hangs up her apron and kisses Elliot lightly on the lips.

                    JESSE
          Bye, love! See you later...

She rushes out of the room.

Elliot takes a few steps into the living room, coffee cup in hand. He looks around.

ELLIOT
She's right. This place *is* a dump!

He starts picking up the comics, but his nature quickly reasserts itself. By the fourth book, he starts reading them, and soon he is on the couch, reading comics.

EXT. SANTA BARBARA - DAY
Jesse's car enters downtown Santa Barbara. It is an older part of town, with a few scattered stone buildings and an air of immobility. This feeling is reinforced by the fact that there are very few people around.

The car enters a main street and heads towards a conservative looking brownstone building which is the headquarters of...

EXT. OCEAN SAVINGS - DAY
The building is set back from the street, with a small tree-lined parking lot in the front. A GOLDEN SIGN at the entrance proudly proclaims the name of the Institution, and the fact that it was established in 1885. The building looks deserted. There are only a couple of cars on the lot.

Jesse drives into the parking lot, and parks her car.

She then walks to the entrance, gets a set of keys from her pocketbook and enters.

INT. OCEAN SAVINGS - MAIN HALL - DAY

The Savings Bank's main hall is reminiscent of Grand Central Station. It is very big and rather gloomy with its lights off. Three large stone pillars reach to the ceiling. On them are posters advertising various financial services. On the wall in front of the customer area, a huge, old-fashioned clock marks the time.

Jesse crosses the hall. The SOUND OF HER FOOTSTEPS on the marbled floor reverberates in the silence.

She reaches a carpeted corridor leading to a series of offices. She calls.

                    JESSE
          Mr. Bennett!

MR. BENNETT comes out of one of the offices. He is a tall and thin man, dressed in a suit that looks a little too large. He has a droopy face, and his plump mouth occasionally makes a masticating motion when he smiles, which reminds one of a rabbit.

                    BENNETT
          Ah, Jessica, you're here. Good! Come with me,
          we have a lot of work to do.

He takes Jesse to an elevator.

INT. OCEAN SAVINGS - ELEVATOR - DAY

Bennett presses the down button. While the elevator is in motion, he explains.

                    BENNET
We need to find all the back-up files of our
existing clients. Some of them are pretty old...

                    JESSE
                 (flippantly)
The clients or the records?

Her small joke draws a blank stare of incomprehension
from Bennett. He hands her a sheet of paper.

                    BENNETT
            I've prepared a list here. I'll start at the
            beginning, and you'll take the end. I hope that
            between the two of us, we can get most of these
            done today. The examiners are coming on
            Wednesday. We have to be ready by then.

The elevator stops with a CLANGING NOISE. The
doors slide open and reveal the Archives Room.

INT. OCEAN SAVINGS - ARCHIVES ROOM - DAY
It is a large room with bare concrete walls and stark
electric lights. The room is furnished with rows and rows
of black metal shelves, labeled by year. On the shelves,
there are cardboard boxes, filed in alphabetical order.

Bennett points at a small desk located by the elevator. It
is covered with computer print-outs.

                    BENNETT
        In case you need to check the balances, I've
        brought down copies of the general ledgers.
        Now, let's get cracking.

He then looks at his list and walks down an aisle.

Jesse stands there for a second, then looks at the last
name on the list.

                     JESSE
        Zweig, G. 1928... Hmm. It should be that way.

After some hesitation, she walks to a shelf and grabs a
file.

CLOSE-UP on the file.

                  DISSOLVE TO:

CAMERA PANS BACK to reveal Jesse sitting on a step
ladder no longer looking as neat as she did when she
walked into the Archives. A few hours have gone by. A
large stack of files lies on the floor next to the ladder.

She has a file spread on her knees. She grabs a pile of
papers, and starts leafing through them.

She coughs because of the dust and fireproof powder
that floats off the documents. She puts the file aside, and
makes a mark on her list.

                            JESSE
                       (sounding tired)
                 OK, Mr. Strickland, that's it for you! Now, on
                 to Stricker, J.

Jesse moves the ladder sideways to a row labeled
"1932," and grabs another, bulging file.
She opens it, then starts checking the documents.

Suddenly, a large, brown envelope slips out of the file
and falls to the floor. Jesse bends over and picks it up.

                            JESSE
                 What's this?

She opens the envelope, sticks her hand in and pulls
out...

JESSE'S POV - A STACK OF $100 BILLS
that cause her eyes to open wide.

She hastily stashes the bank notes back into the envelope. She sits back up on the ladder, slightly flustered.
She again peers nervously into the envelope and takes
another look at

JESSE'S POV - THE BANK NOTES AND ANOTHER
PILE OF DOCUMENTS

Carefully casting a glance around her, she pulls out...

JESSE'S POV - THE DOCUMENTS
which are yellow and stiff with age. These are forms
requesting the opening of an account. There is also a

receipt for $250,000, dated June, 22, 1932 and signature specimens in the name of...

CLOSE-UP - "WILFRID STRICKER"

She closes the cover of the file in her lap to read the name that is on it. It is not that of Wilfrid Stricker, but is that of...

CLOSE-UP - "JAMES STRICKER"

She thinks hard for a while.

> JESSE
> All that money! It's impossible. The officer who opened the account must have made a mistake. He must have registered the deposit in the wrong name... under the wrong Stricker. But why all these bills!?

Then, reaching a decision, she puts the envelope back in the file.

Jesse walks over to the desk with the computer print-outs. She grabs one dated 1932, and starts flipping through it.

She looks for a $250,000 deposit under the name of "Wilfrid Stricker," but...

JESSE'S POV - THERE IS NO ACCOUNT UNDER THAT NAME.

Then, she looks for the "James Stricker" account. But, it only shows little activity in the account, none with the amount of $250,000.

Jesse looks into CAMERA, her eyes reflecting the germ of an idea.

Wanting to make sure that the money is truly unaccounted for, she sorts through a few other printouts in the stack.

Jesse hurriedly walks back to the aisle. She again pulls the documents out of the brown envelope and starts reading them closely.

> JESSE
> A prospector... He came to open an account. His life savings probably... Then, he must have gone away. Never came back... Otherwise they'd have found out about the mistake and corrected it.
> (grabbing a handful of bills)
> All this cash has been sitting in the wrong file all that time. Nobody even knows of it. What if... No, I couldn't. It would be illegal...

She takes another look at the bills, bites her lower lip and frowns intensely.

> JESSE
> Besides, it wouldn't work... I'd need a name and address that couldn't be connected with me. Unless... Yes...

Suddenly, another idea flashes through her mind. She grabs the envelope and buries it in her pocketbook.

Jesse walks over to another aisle. There, she locates Bennett.

                    JESSE
     Mr. Bennett, I need to go upstairs for a minute.
     I'll be right back.

Bennett acknowledges her with a gesture and nods his approval.

INT. OCEAN SAVINGS - ELEVATOR - DAY
Jesse rides the elevator, her pocketbook held pressed tight against her. She makes small movements of impatience, licking her lips, etc., and looks like she is thinking hard.

INT. OCEAN SAVINGS - MAIN HALL - DAY
Jesse crosses the hall and goes to one of the desks in the client reception area. She opens a drawer and takes out several forms that read...

CLOSE-UP - "Opening of Account," "Signature Cards," etc.

Jesse stops for a second, looks around, then grabs the telephone and starts dialing.

INT. APARTMENT - DAY
Elliot is still on the couch, reading comics. The phone RINGS.

He gets up and answers it. It's Jesse.

                    ELLIOT
          Hi, hon! Still at work?

INT. OCEAN SAVINGS - MAIN HALL - DAY
                    JESSE
          Yes. I need to ask you something. Don't ask me
          any questions right now, but it's important. Do
          you and Cliff still own that warehouse that you
          used to run your mail order business on week-
          ends?

                    ELLIOT (V.O.)
          Sure. But why do you ask?

                    JESSE
          I can't tell you right now. Just give me the
          address... and your Social Security number too.

INT. APARTMENT - DAY

                    ELLIOT
          You're not doing something crazy, are you?
                    (beat)
          OK, OK. It's 1231 Wendigo Avenue...

INT. OCEAN SAVINGS - MAIN HALL - DAY
Jesse starts filling in the forms.

                    JESSE
          OK. Thanks, love. Don't worry, I'll explain
          everything later.

She hangs up and keeps writing. She fills more forms, stamps some of them.

When her job is finished, she looks down at...

JESSE'S POV - THE COMPLETED FORMS
which show the opening of an account in the name of a MR. R. FLUSH, residing at the address given by Elliot, and with an initial deposit of $250,000.

Jesse smiles. She takes a new envelope out of the drawer, and transfers the money and the forms to it.

She then goes to the front door and leaves.

EXT. OCEAN SAVINGS - DAY
Jesse walks to the outside "night" deposit slot, and drops the envelope.

She stands there for a second, pensive, and then walks back into the building.

INT. APARTMENT - DAY
Elliot stands in the middle of the living room, a comic book still in hand. His expression is a mixture of intense worry and utter surprise.

                    ELLIOT
          You did what? We can go to jail for something
          like this!

JESSE
(calmly)
No, we won't.

ELLIOT
(increasingly excited)
Yes, we will! I don't want us to go to jail! You
don't know what jail is all about! It's *awful*!

He grabs a comic book.

ELLIOT
Hyper Man went to jail–he was framed–and they
showed how terrible it is. There were those
thugs who beat him up, then he almost got
raped, then...

JESSE
(slightly surprised)
They don't do that in comics.

ELLIOT
Yes, today, they do. It helps the sales. Look.

He hands her one of the comics.

JESSE
(eyes wide open)
My God, you're right! It's disgusting!

ELLIOT
(masochistic)
Well, that's what going to happen to us now!

Jesse throws the book away.

                    JESSE
               (calmly)
          Now, listen to me instead of indulging in Hyper
          Man rape fantasies. First, we haven't really
          stolen any money. Nobody even knew that this
          money existed. The guy just disappeared. He
          was 62 at the time. If he were alive today, he'd
be   114! So we're safe.

                    ELLIOT
          But you forged the documents!

Jesse feels uncomfortable, possibly even more so than
Elliot. She is even more aware than he, of the risk in
what she's done. However, she has had time to consider
the ramifications of her actions.

When next she speaks, it is with a degree of assurance in
her voice, although an acute observer would wonder if
she isn't trying to convince herself as much as Elliot.

                    JESSE
          OK, so I did. I opened the account in the
          shop's name instead of using yours or mine.
          That way they can't connect it with us. If I had
          suddenly deposited $250,000, someone would
          get suspicious.
               (a beat)
          Besides, we won't touch the money. We'll just
          collect the interest on it. That way, everybody is

JESSE (cont'd)
happy. The bank gets to keep the cash and, at ten
percent a year, it will bring us an extra $25,000.
(another beat)
Even after taxes, that still means we'll be able to
afford to buy a house!

Elliot remains unconvinced. Although his suspicions
have not disappeared, he has learned from past experi-
ences that, in matters of money, Jesse is always right.
This assuages his fears, and his mind starts turning over
the implications of what Jesse has done. He discovers
that the idea of being rich has a considerable appeal. He
can't quite, however, bring himself to believe it.

ELLIOT
What if there's an audit?

JESSE
Well, the papers will stand any examination.
Auditors don't normally go visit warehouses or
check drivers' licenses. They'll have a name and
a social security number, and that's all they'll
care about...
(a beat)
Besides, auditors look for money going *out*, not
money coming *in*. No, I tell you, we'll just get
the interest checks in the mail, pay our taxes
and everything will be OK.

ELLIOT
(dreaming)
That'd be great!

JESSE
(very positive)
It *is* great! It's the opportunity we always
dreamed of.

ELLIOT
(as an afterthought)
Shouldn't we tell Cliff? After all, you used the
shop's name, and half of it belongs to him.

JESSE
(guiltily)
I guess we'll have to.

ELLIOT
Oh, I'm sure he won't tell, and he won't mind.
In fact, he wanted to have the shop repainted,
but we couldn't afford it. Now, we can...

JESSE
(interrupting firmly)
Now we can save some money so that we can
make a downpayment on a nice house.

ELLIOT
(conciliatory)
OK, hon.

He really gets into the spirit of it. The prospect of being
rich has now become an actuality.

ELLIOT
Why don't we celebrate? I'll take you to that
new fancy French place that opened in town.

JESSE
(smiling)
OK, let's celebrate *avec* style, as they say!
Tomorrow, I'd like to start looking at houses...

Elliot makes a show of bringing Jesse's jacket and ushering her through the door.

EXT. APARTMENT COMPLEX - DUSK
Elliot and Jesse go down the stairs, arm and arm, looking very happy.

EXT. SANTA BARBARA - DAY
Elliot and Jesse, accompanied by a bubbly-looking woman, a real estate agent, are looking at a house.

JESSE
What do you think, honey?

ELLIOT
Ho-hum.

EXT. SANTA BARBARA - ANOTHER PART OF TOWN - DAY
Very much the same scene. This time, it is a male real estate agent and a much nicer place. Elliot looks at a *very large* room.

ELLIOT
That'd be perfect for my comics.

EXT. SANTA BARBARA - OUTSIDE OF TOWN - DAY

This time, Elliot and Jesse are looking at a small ranch. Jesse looks ecstatic.

> JESSE
>
> Now, that's what I call a home!

EXT. SANTA BARBARA - A CAR SHOW ROOM - DAY

Elliot points at a white Mercedes.

> ELLIOT
>
> Wouldn't that be nice?...

> JESSE
>
> (smiling)
>
> If I showed up at work in that, it would be a bit suspicious, don't you think?

CLOSE-UP on a fleeting look of fear that flashes across Elliot's face.

EXT. SANTA BARBARA - OUTSIDE A DEPART-MENT STORE - DAY

Elliot is watching the street scene. Jesse comes out of the store, wearing a very attractive, fashionable dress.

> JESSE
>
> (modeling)
>
> You like it?

Elliot whistles.

INT. ROYAL FLUSH COMICS - DAY

Elliot sits behind the counter, reading a comic book. The shop is empty, except for a lone CUSTOMER.

We HEAR tires screeching. He gets up, goes to the window and sees

ELLIOT'S POV - Cliff just parking his beat-up, old Chevy outside the shop.

Cliff comes in, an envelope in hand.

> CLIFF
>
> Hi, Elliot! I dropped by the warehouse this morning, and there was a funny letter. It comes from Jesse's company, and it's addressed to Mr. R. Flush. I can't make any sense of it. Know anything about it?

He hands the letter to Elliot, who looks very pale.

> ELLIOT
>
> A letter... let me see...

Elliot starts reading. After the first few lines, his face drops.

> ELLIOT
>
> I knew it! I knew it!

> CLIFF
>
> What is it?

40

ELLIOT
(very close to panicking)
They want to see me! That's it! We're going to
jail! I told her we couldn't get away with it!

Cliff grabs the letter and looks at it.

CLIFF
I don't understand any of it. This looks like an
invitation from their chairman to a board
meeting. Where's the harm? Why is it addressed
to us in the first place, and who's this Flush guy
anyway?

Elliot turns towards Cliff, looking embarrassed.

ELLIOT
(pointing at a chair)
I think you'd better sit down. I have a story to
tell you... But first...

Elliot walks to the Customer and puts a hand on his
shoulder.

ELLIOT
Sorry. You have to go. We're closing.

CUSTOMER
(surprised)
Closing? But it's only 11 a.m.

ELLIOT
(never at a loss for words)
Cliff here just heard that his mother died. We
have to close. Sorry.

He starts ushering the Customer towards the door.

CUSTOMER
(obviously acquainted with Cliff's
family story)
His mother? But she died three years ago!

ELLIOT
(pushing the customer through the door)
Cliff only learned about it today. Mail's terrible.
Now, go!

He SLAMS the door in the Customer's face.

The Customer stands outside, waving a couple of comics.

CUSTOMER
(through the door)
Wait. I didn't pay for my comics!

Elliot turns the "Open" sign over to "Closed."

ELLIOT
It's OK. His mother would have wanted you to
have them. Goodbye!

The Customer disgusted, walks away.

Cliff has watched the entire scene bemusedly and with a fair amount of stoicism.

CLIFF
I hope your story's worth it. I hate people who make fun of my poor, late mother.

Elliot, very serious, almost grim, points at a chair.

ELLIOT
I told you to sit down.

Cliff does, intrigued.

DISSOLVE TO:

Elliot is finishing the story.

ELLIOT
...The thing is, we meant to tell you, and then I guess we kind of forgot...

Cliff gets up and towers over Elliot. He waves his arms, while he loudly expresses his indignation.

CLIFF
(outraged)
Kind of forgot! You're ruining my perfectly honest and, so far, untainted business reputation for a kooky embezzling scheme, and you say you "kind of forgot" to tell me! Oh, that's grand! That's really grand!

ELLIOT
(conciliatory)
I'm sorry. We really meant to. Besides, we
didn't embezzle any money. And Jesse said
there'd be no risk...

CLIFF
(dangerously calm)
Fine. What did Jesse say we do when you get
invited to the board meeting?

Elliot starts pacing around the room, becoming more and
more agitated. For perhaps the first time in his life, he
realizes that he is stuck in a situation that he can't just
ignore.

ELLIOT
I don't know. I just don't know.

CLIFF
(shouting)
Then, why don't you stop pacing and ask her!
We have to get out of the mess that you two
idiots cooked up!

Elliot stops pacing. He hesitantly goes to the telephone
and starts dialing.

INT. OCEAN SAVINGS - JESSE'S DESK - DAY
Jesse works at her desk in the customer area. The telephone RINGS. She answers.

JESSE
Good morning, Ocean Savings. May I help you?

ELLIOT (V.O.)
Honey, you have to get over here quick. We've
got to talk. There's a letter...

JESSE
(frowning)
Elliot, is that you? What's wrong?

INT. ROYAL FLUSH COMICS – DAY

ELLIOT
I told you! We got a letter from your Bank. They
want to see me! What are we going to do?

INT. OCEAN SAVINGS - JESSE'S DESK – DAY

JESSE
Right now, nothing. Stay at the shop. I'll be
right there. I'll take the rest of the day off..

She hangs up the phone, remains pensive a moment and
quietly looks around. Then she gets up and walks away.

INT. ROYAL FLUSH COMICS - BACKROOM - DAY
Most of the room is filled with the shop inventory. It's
definitely a "no-frills" room. A sink with a pile of un-
washed cups sits off to one side. Elliot, Jesse and Cliff
are sitting at a table in the center of the room.

Jesse reads the letter. She is ignoring the moaning conversation of Elliot and Cliff.

ELLIOT
What are we going to do? What are we going to
do?

CLIFF
I want to warn both of you that I'm not going to
jail because you suddenly decided to take a
shortcut to the American Dream.

JESSE
(finishing the letter)
Well, that doesn't look particularly threatening
to me. In fact, it's rather charming. It's from
Mr. Feller, our chairman. He says that you're
one of the newest and largest depositors they
have. So, he's inviting you to a board meeting.
They want you to see for yourself how well they
manage your funds, and why they deserve your
confidence.

She puts the letter flat on the table, and looks calmly at
the two men.
JESSE
Frankly, I think you've both been overreacting.
This looks like standard banking practice to
me...

ELLIOT
(suddenly feeling *much* better)
You mean we can just ignore the whole thing?

46

                              JESSE
                         (thinking aloud)
No, we shouldn't. I don't think it would be
wise...
                         (a beat)
It might draw questions. Somebody who has just
invested $250,000 in a small Savings Bank is
not likely to pass up an opportunity to see what
they're doing with his money...

She reaches a sudden decision and points at Elliot.

                              JESSE
No, you have to go.

                              ELLIOT
                         (with a stricken look again)
Me! I don't want to go! I can't go! Besides,
they'll know me...

                              JESSE
                         (laughing)
No, they won't! Feller doesn't even know you
exist. And I don't think he's the type to hang
around comics shops!
                         (beat)
In any event, you won't be going as Elliot
Martin, comic book dealer and part-time writer,
but as Mr. Roger Flush, a sharp, big-time, city
investor! The only thing you need to do is go
there, impress them and convince them that you
are who you pretend to be. That's all.

ELLIOT
(overwhelmed)
That's *all*?!

JESSE
Sure. If you don't ask stupid questions everything will be fine. You can do it. They'll
swallow it hook, line and sinker. Then, no more
problems!

Both men consider Jesse's remarks for a moment. Finally, Elliot speaks.

ELLIOT
Why Roger Flush?

JESSE
(dismissing the remark with a gesture)
I don't know. Roger, Raymond... It doesn't
matter.

CLIFF
How about Robert?

Elliot snaps his fingers.

ELLIOT
Yeah, Robert Flush... I like it! I could dress like
Tony Stork did in "Captain Iron."

Elliot starts foraging for a "Captain Iron" comic book to
prove his point. Unable to find one, he gives up and begins to act out the parts of the characters he describes.

ELLIOT
(aristocratically)
"Get my suit ready, Alfred. Captain Iron is needed!"

CLIFF
(thinking)
No, I see you better as Bruce Payne...

ELLIOT
(excitedly)
Yeah, "Catman," that's it!
(humming a jingle)
"Caaatmaan! Caatmaan!"
(making his voice sound like a
TV announcer)
"The world knows him as Catman, The Dark Avenger of the Night. In reality he is Bruce Payne, playboy millionaire..."

Jesse watches the scene with a slightly confused look on her face.

JESSE
What *are* you two talking about?

ELLIOT
Comics. Bruce Payne is the secret identity of "Catman," the Dark Avenger of the Night... He's a real neat character–the perfect role model for the part of Robert Flush.

JESSE
Good. Then, you need a new suit and a...

CLIFF
(interrupting)
White, the suit.

JESSE
(paying no attention)
...a haircut. Besides, you've been needing a haircut for a while. OK, let's get this show on the road.

INT. SANTA BARBARA - AN EXPENSIVE CLOTH-ING STORE - DAY
Elliot inside a booth, tries on a beautiful, white suit. He walks out of the booth.

ELLIOT
Ta-da!

Jesse looks very impressed.

JESSE
Wow!

She steps forwards and touches the fabric.

JESSE
This looks incredible! Your own mother wouldn't recognize you in this suit...

ELLIOT
I don't recognize me in this suit!

INT. SANTA BARBARA - HAIR SALON - DAY
Elliot is getting a stylish haircut and a manicure.

EXT. SANTA BARBARA - HAIR SALON - DAY
Jesse meets Elliot outside of the salon. She carries several department store bags. She looks him over.

                    JESSE
     Nice. Real nice.

She pats her bags.

                    JESSE
     I bought you a hair color spray. We'll add some
     silver sparkle to those temple of yours! It's good
     camouflage just in case, and it will help you
     look the part.
          (beat)
     I've also got some other stuff here, like
     sunglasses and jewelry, that you'll need. With
     all that, and the new suit, you'll look
     magnificent.

INT. ROYAL FLUSH COMICS - BACKROOM - DAY
Jesse's purchases are neatly piled against the wall. Elliot turns towards Cliff.

                    ELLIOT
     I think we have everything we need here...
          (embarrassed)
     There's one other thing, though. You see, the
     way we figured it, Flush can't just walk in... He
     needs to arrive... I mean, he...

JESSE
(interrupting)
What Elliot is trying to say is that we'd like to
borrow your car.

CLIFF
(puzzled)
My old Chevy? Sure. But why?

Elliot looks like he is anticipating an explosion.

ELLIOT
No, not your Chevy, Cliff. Your *other* car.

Cliff pales. His eyes widen.

CLIFF
My *other* car? Oh, no! No, no, no, no! Nobody
borrows my other car. I don't even trust myself
with it...

JESSE
(begging)
Cliff, we need a car that matches Flush's style.
Your car is the only one that fits the bill.

ELLIOT
I promise I'll take good care of it. It's only for a
few miles. You want to help us, don't you?

CLIFF
(stubbornly)
Not with my car.

Elliot attempts to sweet talk Cliff.

                    ELLIOT
          Listen, if we pull it off... You know how much
          you and I talked about redecorating the shop?
          Well, I promise that, if all goes well, we'll
          repaint the whole place. We'll invite big-name
          artists to come and do autograph parties...

Cliff starts to weaken. He looks coyly at Elliot.

                    CLIFF
          Can we get the guy that draws "Dribble" in the
          Times?

                    ELLIOT
                (without thinking)
          No way! I hate "Dribble!" The stuff stinks! That
          guy is a hack...

Elliot looks at Jesse who is grimacing at him, trying to
make him shut up. He realizes what he's doing and continues in the same breath.

                    ELLIOT
          ...but of course, if you want him, it's OK with
          me.

Cliff beams happily.

                    ELLIOT
                (to himself, shaking his head forlornly)
          "Dribble..."

CLIFF
But, what if something happens to her...

Elliot moves closer to him and puts his arm around his friend's shoulder.

ELLIOT
Nothing will. Didn't I take good care of your comics collection when you went away for a vacation two years ago?

CLIFF
Yeah, but it's not the same...

Jesse duplicates Elliot's move. The two of them now surround Cliff.

JESSE
Cliff, we really need that car. Elliot and I spent all our savings to equip him in style. We don't have any more money, and we don't dare touch the money in the bank. This is our last chance. Please, Cliff, we're all in it, now.

ELLIOT
(desperate)
I tell you what. You know my collection of "Silver Surfer" that you always wanted?
I'll make a deal with you. I'll give you the entire set if you let me have the car.

                    CLIFF
              (moved, for the first time)
         You can't do that!
              (a beat)
         Those comics are worth a fortune!

                    ELLIOT
              (nobly)
         Yes, I can. They're my comics.

Cliff gives in with a sigh.

                    CLIFF
         OK, you win. You can have the car.
              (a beat)
         But keep your "Silver Surfer."

                    ELLIOT
         Great! Let's go!

Elliot immediately walks out of the room.

                    JESSE
         Where?

                    ELLIOT (O.S.)
         To the warehouse. That's where Cliff keeps
         his car.

EXT. WAREHOUSE - DUSK
The warehouse is an anonymous, grey-looking building,
located in a rather shabby street on the outskirts of the

town. Nothing identifies it. On the front, there is a metal door with some junk mail stuffed under it. Cliff's Chevy and Jesse's Toyota are parked in front of the building.

Elliot and Jesse stand on the sidewalk, waiting for Cliff. Cliff gets out of his car, walks to the door, unlocks and opens it. He enters. The others follow him into...

INT. WAREHOUSE - DUSK
The inside of the warehouse is starkly lit by neon lights. The walls are bare. The decor looks like a cross between the backroom of "Royal Flush Comics" and a garage.

Boxes of comic books are laying around the concrete floor, next to various, assorted car tools. Off to one side, there is a large, wooden worktable covered by car magazines and car parts.

On one side of the room, there is a large, sliding metal garage door. Cliff's "fancy" car is in the middle of the room, covered with a white, canvas tarpaulin.

Cliff gently removes the tarp, revealing the car beneath. It is a beautifully preserved, 1920s or 1930s English automobile. Its chrome and engine shine and sparkle under the bright glare of the neon.
He looks at the car with love. He sighs and turns towards Elliot and Jesse.

                    CLIFF
          There she is! A beauty! The exact copy of the
          car Patrick Macnee used to drive in "The
          Avengers!"

Jesse approaches the car and passes her hand over the chassis. She walks around it.

JESSE
It's fantastic! You've done an amazing job.

Cliff follows Jesse, discreetly rubbing away her finger-prints with a clean cloth.

CLIFF
I spent six years working on her...

Meanwhile, Elliot walks around the warehouse. Taking on the role of Flush is starting to transform his carriage into that of a more assured person. He lights up a cigarette and puffs on it a few times. He then adopts a dramatic stance, and playfully starts speaking in comic book cliches.

ELLIOT
With this car, let the world beware! Robert Flush has arrived!

EXT. WAREHOUSE - DAY
ESTABLISHING SHOT of the warehouse. We HEAR BLARING MUSIC from "Star Wars" or "Batman."

INT. WAREHOUSE - DAY
Cliff, rag in hand, finishes polishing the car. On the workbench next to him is a tape deck. He calls:

CLIFF
OK, Elliot!

CLIFF (cont'd)
(almost tenderly)
She's ready for you.

CLOSE-UP on Elliot's feet, inside impeccable, white boots.

CAMERA PANS UPWARD AND BACK, to reveal the rest of Elliot in his Flush attire–white suit, lavender shirt, expensive jewelry, Porsche sunglasses, etc. He looks pristine and absolutely superb. Cliff's mouth drops.

CLIFF
Elliot, old pal, is that you!?

ELLIOT
(haughtily)
The Dark Avenger of the Night prepares to do battle!

CLIFF
But it's daylight out there!

ELLIOT
Us avengers ain't bothered by that!

Elliot walks majestically to the car and gets in. Cliff opens the garage door.

CLOSE-UP on Elliot turning the ignition. The car sputters, then starts smoothly.

EXT. WAREHOUSE - DRIVEWAY - DAY
Cliff stops Elliot as he drives out of the warehouse.

CLIFF
(sounding like a nervous father)
You promise to take good care of her?

Elliot coolly lowers his sunglasses and looks haughtily at Cliff–his "Flush look"–then winks and breaks into his own, charming smile. He gestures at Cliff to come closer.

ELLIOT
Remember what I said about my "Silver Surfer?"

CLIFF
Yes.

ELLIOT
I meant it. They're yours.

Cliff steps back, smiling to himself. Elliot shouts and waves his hand.

ELLIOT
Hi Yo Silver, away!

He floors the gas pedal, leaving a cloud of dust and the smell of burning rubber in his wake.

EXT. SANTA BARBARA - DAY
Elliot drives along the streets with panache. The car re-acts smoothly to his commands. The traffic is moderate, typical of an average, mid-week morning. His route takes him to...

<u>EXT. OCEAN SAVINGS - DAY</u>
ESTABLISHING SHOT of the building. CAMERA
PULLS IN on a window on the second floor.

<u>INT. OCEAN SAVINGS - FELLER'S OFFICE - DAY</u>
The office of Ocean Savings' chairman is plush, yet conservative. It is furnished with items made by local arti-
sans, reminding one that we are in the West, and that
local tradition is strong.

MR. FELLER sits in a comfortable looking, brown
leather armchair behind a beautiful, polished wood desk.
He is a small, plump man, with a round, honest face and
little hair. He speaks with a regional drawl, and likes to
accompany his speech with gestures of familiarity. His
dress is mildly conservative, except for the white cow-
boy hat that is presently hanging on the rack near the
door.

There are five other people in the room. One is Bennett.
The other three are local business people, including a
middle-aged woman. Together they comprise the Board
of Directors of Ocean Savings. Feller addresses the others.

                    FELLER
          I asked you all to come a little early, because, in
          conformity with our recent policies, I've taken
          the liberty of inviting our latest jumbo depositor
          to today's meeting. His name is, mmm...

He looks at a sheet of paper.

FELLER

...Mr. R. Flush, professional investor. I see here
that his local address is a business address. His
home address appears to be in Los Angeles.
                    (a beat; he looks around the room)
Mr. Flush has recently invested $250,000 with
our bank. I am certain that he must be a gentleman of considerable resources. He could
probably become a valuable addition to our
community. I hope, therefore, that we will do
our best to impress him with...

He notices a question on the face of MRS. WILSON, the
only woman Board Member.

FELLER

Yes, Joanna?

MRS. WILSON

Has anyone met Mr. Flush?

FELLER

No. It would appear that his account was opened
by mail. I'm sure that we are all very curious
about him.

EXT. OCEAN SAVINGS - PARKING LOT - DAY

Elliot zooms into the parking lot. He stops the car, tires
SCREECHING, in front of a surprised guard.

INT. OCEAN SAVINGS - FELLER'S OFFICE - DAY

Everyone has heard the SCREECH. Feller and two other
Board Members go to the window and see

FELLER'S POV - ELLIOT JUMPING OUT OF THE
CAR WITH AGILITY.

EXT. OCEAN SAVINGS - PARKING LOT - DAY
Elliot throws the keys to the guard. From now on, when
Elliot plays the part of Flush, he speaks with a voice that
sounds more sophisticated and worldly than his natural
voice.

> ELLIOT
> Have my car parked, will you? I'm late for the
> Board meeting.

He walks into the lobby, leaving behind him a completely bewildered guard.

INT. OCEAN SAVINGS - FELLER'S OFFICE - DAY
Elliot's entrance has had a tremendous effect upon Feller
and the other Board Members. Feller looks impressed,
and almost meek as he says:

> FELLER
> I think Mr. Flush has just arrived!

INT. OCEAN SAVINGS - BOARD ROOM - DAY
The Board Room is just that. A large, oval, mahogany
table, with green desk pads, and seven comfortable
chairs take up most of the space. In a corner, there is a
smaller table with a jug of coffee and cups. Portraits of
past bank chairmen adorn the wooden, paneled walls.
Feller, followed by the other Board Members, walks in
through a side door. A few seconds later, Elliot enters

the room theatrically, through the main set of double doors.

Feller walks up to him and shakes his hand.

>   FELLER
>   Ah, Mr. Flush! I'm pleased to meet you! Let me
>   introduce myself. I'm Stanton Feller, Chairman
>   of Ocean Savings.

He then proceeds to introduce Bennett, who also comes up to shake Elliot's hand.

>   FELLER
>   This is my second-in-command, Avery
>   Bennett.

>   BENNETT
>   How do you do?

Elliot nods. The other Board Members follow on cue.

>   FELLER
>   This charming lady is Miss Joanna Wilson, of
>   Wilson's, our town's largest department store.

>   MRS. WILSON
>   How do you do?

>   FELLER
>   This is William Gardner of the law firm of
>   Gardner & Mitchell.

GARDNER

Pleased to meet you.

FELLER
(smiling)
And, last but not least, this is Bud Kleinman of
the Kleinman Cement Works Co.
(a beat)
You might have heard of them in Los Angeles.
Bud has been fairly active in the real estate
market.

KLEINMAN
(boisterously)
Stan is too kind. Nice to meet you, Mr. Flush.
Welcome aboard... a board!

KLEINMAN laughs. No one else does.

Elliot takes a small step backward. He puts his arms out
in an all-encompassing gesture and breaks into his most
charming smile.

ELLIOT
Thank you, Gentlemen...
(making a slight bow towards
Mrs. Wilson)
...and Lady. I was delighted to receive your
invitation. Let me reassure you, that it is indeed
a pleasure to be here with you today.

Elliot then makes a small tour of the room, looking at
each of the portraits as he passes it.

The Board Members stand silently in a group. They look at each other, unsure of what to say next.

Elliot again stands in front of them, and continues.

> ELLIOT
> I trust that some of you, in turn, may have heard of me, or Flush Investments?

The Board Members look embarrassed. None of them have. Elliot looks genuinely contrite.

> ELLIOT
> I'm sorry. I assume too much...

> FELLER
> (smiling)
> You must make allowances for us, Mr. Flush. Santa Barbara may not be the financial capital of the world, but I think you'll find that we're not hayseeds either!

> ELLIOT
> (conciliatory)
> Please, don't mention it! I understand... And, don't call me Mr. Flush... All my friends call be Robert...
> (struck with a flash of inspiration)
> ...or "Royal."

> KLEINMAN
> "Royal?" "Royal" Flush? Oh, boy! I've got to introduce you to my poker pals!

ELLIOT
(as if taking them into a confidence)
Yes, a rather fancy surname, I agree. But, it's
one that I inherited in my youth, years ago in
Monte Carlo. It brought me luck, and then stuck.
I liked it, so I kept it.

The Board Members appear impressed in spite of them-
selves. Elliot feigns ignorance of the effect that he is
having. He is starting to enjoy himself immensely.

FELLER
(unable to suppress his awe)
Monte Carlo? I see...

ELLIOT
(falsely surprised)
You know Monte Carlo?

FELLER
(trying to extricate himself)
Well, not exactly... No... I always meant to go...

ELLIOT
(pressing his advantage quickly)
Beautiful place! I keep a house there... More like
an estate, actually. I like to go back now and
then.

The other Board Members visibly start warming up to
Elliot.

                         KLEINMAN
                     (aside to Gardner)
              I thought "Monte Carlo" was a car...

GARDNER shrugs, ignores the remark and takes the
opportunity to ask Elliot a question.

                         GARDNER
              Does your business often take you to Europe,
              Mr. Flush?

                         ELLIOT
                         (vague)
              I have investments all over the world,
              Mr. Gardner.
                         (a beat)
              You could say, I lead a "worldly" life!

Elliot smiles at his own joke. He pulls a beautiful, gold
cigarette case out of his pocket, nonchalantly flips it
open and offers the imported cigarettes around the room.
Kleinman takes three. Elliot makes a show of not noticing, and continues.

                         ELLIOT
              Of course, all this requires a considerable
              amount of traveling. But, it's really very
              exciting. Last month, for instance, I was in
              Moscow with...

                         FELLER
                     (interrupting)
              Excuse me... You have investments in Russia?

ELLIOT
(appearing to be concerned)
Perhaps I've said too much. Some of my
investments are, how shall I put it–sensitive. My
friends in Washington are sometimes a bit
overly cautious in the area of security.

Kleinman when he hears the word "Washington," is
quick to smell the potential for profit.

KLEINMAN
(excitedly)
You work with Washington? Government
contracts, that kind of thing?

ELLIOT
(laughing)
My dear Mr. Kleinman, in our profession, who
doesn't work with Washington?

KLEINMAN
Of course, of course...
(a beat)
Hey, Royal, maybe you could put in a good
word for me with your buddies?

Gardner embarrassed, interrupts Kleinman.

GARDNER
I was wondering why a man with your
connections, would come to Santa Barbara to
invest?

ELLIOT

Frankly, I like your city. It reminds me of Monte
Carlo. Although my California affairs keep me
mostly in Los Angeles, I'd like to spend some
time here.
(a beat)
Besides, it's only a small sum of money... Call it
a fancy. I probably won't even use it.

KLEINMAN
(impressed)
Boy, oh boy!

Elliot feels he has now put up enough of a show, and
wants to wrap it up.

ELLIOT

But enough of this. I'm keeping you away from
your duties.

FELLER

No, no! Not at all! This is extremely interesting,
Mr. ...er... Robert... er...

ELLIOT
(relishing his power)
Royal!

FELLER

...er, yes, Royal. For a time now, I've been
thinking...

Feller tries to channel his thoughts. He starts pacing in a small circle, his hands behind his back. His tone becomes a bit pedantic.

> FELLER
> ...You see Royal, savings banks have been under a great deal of pressure lately. Interest rates have gone up, then down. New regulations have been passed by the government. Our business today requires a great deal more sophistication than it did when I joined this bank, almost 40 years ago.
> (a beat)
> I've been thinking that we need new, aggressive blood on the board...

MRS. WILSON interrupts politely, but firmly, slightly deflating Feller's balloon.

> MRS. WILSON
> Stanton, before you go on, I have a question for Mr. Flush.

> FELLER
> By all means, Joanna.

> MRS. WILSON
> (to Elliot)
> Tell me, Mr. Flush. If I may be so bold as to ask. You're obviously a very rich man. Where have you made your fortune? Oil? Futures? The stock market?

Elliot looks calculatingly at the woman. She is a no-nonsense type of person, looking grand and yet extremely sharp at the same time.

He is momentarily at a loss for a good answer. Although Mrs. Wilson means no harm with her question, if anyone can cause the scheme to backfire, it is she.

He flashes his most winning smile, and launches himself into what, he hopes, will be a satisfying response.

                    ELLIOT
          A bit of all that, of course...

Suddenly, the answer to his immediate predicament appears to him in a wild flash.

                    ELLIOT (cont'd)
          ...but mostly, comic books.

A LONG SILENCE. Finally:

                    FELLER
                (not understanding)
          Comic books?

Elliot once again feels that he is fully in control of the situation. For the first time, he *really* knows what he is talking about.

When he next speaks, it is as if the *true* Elliot has joined forces with Flush.

ELLIOT

Yes, Comic books! Think about it. Every day, thousands, millions of copies, are sold world-wide. It's a major publishing industry...

KLEINMAN
(interrupting)
But comics are crappy, worthless, trash!

ELLIOT

Not all that worthless today, my friend! Some retail for ten bucks a piece.
(a beat)
Did you know, that a savvy investor could buy the first issue of "Action Comics" for $50 dollars 20 years ago, and today he could sell it for $500,000!

Kleinman gasps.

ELLIOT
(pressing his advantage)
How many other investments give that rate of return? None! And, I haven't even mentioned the merchandising. Toys, cereals, posters, television series... major motion pictures!

Elliot strides towards Feller. He points at the sky.

ELLIOT

Surely, you're familiar with the character that has the big "S" on his chest and wears a red cape?

FELLER
(overwhelmed by Elliot's rhetoric)
Uh... Yes.

ELLIOT
Well, the three movies alone made over
$1 billion!

He leaves time for the figure to sink in. It does, kayoing
their resistance.

ELLIOT
(mysteriously)
I'm sure you can see how someone who owned
even a small percentage of such a valuable property could become very, very rich.

Feller is now completely convinced. Better yet, he has
gained new respect and confidence in Elliot. He addresses him with a tone of friendliness that was previously absent. He now feels comfortable addressing Elliot
as "Royal."

FELLER
Well put, Royal. You sure made a convincing
case. I think I can speak for the whole board...
(casting a glance at Mrs. Wilson)
... when I say, we all learned something today.

KLEINMAN
(to himself)
I sure did. I thought "Monte Carlo" was a
Chevrolet!

Feller is now more eager than ever to persuade Elliot to join their board.

> FELLER
>
> As I was saying, I believe this bank needs new blood, Royal. You're just the type of person I've been looking for. Will you accept a position on our board?

Elliot is flabbergasted. He never expected his charade to have such impressive results. For the first time since he entered the room, he is truly speechless.

Feller mistakes Elliot's silence for hesitancy.

> FELLER
> (sincerely)
> We're not just asking you because of your money, Royal. There's a great deal that a man with your sophistication could bring to this board.

Elliot, much to his surprise, finds himself truly enjoying his "Flush" experience. It is, after all, the first time in his life that he has received so much serious attention. He is very tempted to accept Feller's offer.

> ELLIOT
> I'm truly flattered, Stanton. I don't know if I can...

Feller walks over to Elliot and pats him on the shoulder.

> FELLER
> Of course, you can!

He turns towards the others.

> FELLER
> I suggest that the first official act of today's
> meeting be to formally ratify the board's
> appointment of our new friend and associate.
> > (specifically to Bennett)
> And, Avery, let's make that unanimous!
> > (to everyone)
> Well then, now that that's taken care of, let's get
> to the business at hand.

Everyone takes a place at the table. Bennett passes several pieces of paper around the table.

> FELLER
> The first item on today's agenda is...

CLOSE-UP on Elliot's face, smiling, at ease and happy.

EXT. APARTMENT COMPLEX - DUSK
ESTABLISHING SHOT of the building. CLOSE-UP on Jesse's car parked outside. THE CAMERA PANS to Jesse running up the stairs.

INT. APARTMENT - DUSK
Jesse enters.

> JESSE
> > (anxious)
> How did it go?

Elliot is back in his old clothes laying on the sofa. The only outward clue that things are different, is that instead of reading a comic book, he now reads a copy of "The Wall Street Journal."

ELLIOT
(cool)
Just fine, piece of cake!

Jesse has missed the "Journal" clue.

JESSE
(excited)
What do you mean, "A piece of cake!" What happened? Everybody was buzzing all day at the bank! Did they ask you any questions?

ELLIOT
Of course they did. Where did I make my money? That kind of thing.

JESSE
Well, what did you say?

ELLIOT
I said I made it in comic books.

JESSE
What!

ELLIOT
(having fun)
And they voted me a seat on the board. You work for me now, baby!

Jesse collapses onto a chair.

                         JESSE
          A seat on the Board! I don't believe it!

Elliot gets up, and circles the living room with a dreamy look on his face.

                         ELLIOT
          You know, hon. I think I'm going to like that
          job.

EXT. ROYAL FLUSH COMICS - DAY
Jesse and Elliot stand by the door, an open envelope in hand.

CLOSE-UP on Elliot's hands holding a check for over $7,000.

INT. OCEAN SAVINGS - BOARD ROOM - DAY
Elliot dressed as Flush, sits at the board table. Cigarette in hand, he smiles confidently as he listens.

INT. ROYAL FLUSH COMICS - DAY
Cliff happily supervises a couple of PAINTERS at work on one of the walls.

EXT. SANTA BARBARA - DAY
SUPERIMPOSE - "THREE MONTHS LATER."

Cliff's Chevy is moving ponderously through the traffic.

As it prepares to cross an intersection, a BLACK LIM-OUSINE cuts in front of him, forcing him to slam on the brakes.

INT. CLIFF'S CAR - DAY
Cliff swears and continues on.

EXT. ROYAL FLUSH COMICS - DAY
Cliff makes a left and enters the shopping center where Royal Flush Comics is located.

INT. ROYAL FLUSH COMICS - DAY
Cliff angrily storms into the shop.

                    CLIFF
        The loonies are sure out today! Some jerk in a
        huge limo nearly killed me out there!

Elliot sits behind the counter. He looks cleaner and more assured. He has matured greatly during the past few months. He raises his eyes towards Cliff.

                    ELLIOT
        You've got to be careful out there, buddy!

EXT. SANTA BARBARA - DAY
The Black Limousine is moving through the traffic. CAMERA ZOOMS IN on the Limousine.

INT. LIMOUSINE - DAY
The driver (JOE) is dressed in a black chauffeur's uni-form, that fits him approximately as well as it would a gorilla. His face registers the same amount of intelli-gence.

RAUSCH's voice comes from the back of the car, but we do not yet see its owner. It is a steely voice, that does not manifest much emotion.

                    RAUSCH (O.S.)
        Be more careful, Joe. I don't have time for you
        to get involved in an accident with a local.

                         JOE
        Yes, Mr. Rausch.

EXT. OCEAN SAVINGS - PARKING LOT - DAY
The Limousine pulls into the parking lot, and stops in front of the building entrance. Joe gets out and goes to open the back door.

RAUSCH steps out of the car. He is an impeccably dressed man of average height and build. His features reflect a cold, calculating personality. His whole attitude embodies the ruthlessness that has come to be associated with "Big Business." This man, in other words, is a shark.

INT. OCEAN SAVINGS - MAIN HALL - DAY
Rausch hands his business card to the receptionist.

CLOSE-UP on the card that reads: J. GORDON RAUSCH, PRESIDENT, AMALGAMATED FINAN-CIAL.

INT. OCEAN SAVINGS - FELLER'S OFFICE - DAY
CLOSE-UP on the same card, now being held by a dif-ferent pair of hands.

CAMERA PANS BACK to reveal Feller, studying the card.

FELLER
Amalgamated Financial, hmm... I wonder what they want... Please, tell Mr. Rausch to come in.

Rausch enters the office, led by the secretary. He exhibits a joyless smile, as he offers his hand to Feller. Feller stands up and hands his business card to Rausch.

FELLER
Pleased to meet you, Mr. Rausch. Have a seat.

Rausch sits down. The two men observe each other for an instant. Feller waits patiently for Rausch to begin.

RAUSCH
I'll get right to the point, My company is, as you may know, one of the largest, diversified financial concerns in the country. We've recently decided to expand into the Santa Barbara area. Our past policy has always been to achieve this through mergers and acquisitions...

Feller is not at all happy about the direction of the conversation. He interrupts with a quip that is more than a little serious.

FELLER
...or failing that, unfriendly takeovers! I've read all about your company's practices in "Fortune," Mr. Rausch.

RAUSCH
(disdainful)
I don't have much regard for the press in
general...
(waving his hand in a gesture
of dismissal)
To return to our discussion... We are planning
to build an elite community along the coast. It
would be something like Palm Springs with an
ocean view. Movie stars, politicians,
millionaires, none of the usual riff raff... We're
talking about a half a billion dollar project here,
Feller! We have foreign investors lined up from
here to Bahrain!

FELLER
If you'll excuse my interruption, I'm afraid
I don't see where we fit into your plans,
Mr. Rausch.

Rausch reclines in his seat, brings his hands together,
fingertips touching, and arranges his face into one of his
mirthless smiles.

RAUSCH
We need land, Feller. Prime land. Land such as
that your bank controls through the mortgages it
has been granting since the turn of the century.
(leaning forward)
What I am proposing is a merger of our
interests. You have the land, we have the
resources to develop it. Of course, in a merger
between our two institutions, you and your

RAUSCH (cont'd)
fellow board members would not be forgotten.
We have extremely attractive executive
compensation packages that run...

Feller adopts a poker face and looks at Rausch.

FELLER
If I understand your drift, Mr. Rausch, what you
intend to do is to use some kind of legal
chicanery to appropriate the land of people that
have put their trust in us for all these years!

RAUSCH
They would be compensated, of course...

FELLER
But at what rate?

RAUSCH
One doesn't make an omelet without breaking
some eggs, Feller.

Feller stands up and puts his hands flat on his desk.

FELLER
I'm sorry, Mr. Rausch. We don't have anything
further to discuss. The answer is no.
          (a beat)
I'll have my secretary show you out.

Rausch remains seated. A hint of something unpleasant
creeps into his eyes.

RAUSCH
Perhaps your fellow board members would be
more receptive to my proposal, Feller.

Feller replies with a strength born of conviction.

FELLER
No, Mr. Rausch, they won't! We, at Ocean
Savings, have always considered that it is a
bank's first duty to be at the service of its
community–not to rape its assets for personal
gain... I know I can speak for all of my
colleagues when I say that your scheme will find
no support here. Good-bye, Mr. Rausch.

Rausch remains immobile in his seat. He takes a black,
leather-bound notebook out of his breast pocket and
starts leafing through it.

RAUSCH
I don't think you understand me, Feller. We
want this land.

He starts reading from his book.

RAUSCH
Ackerman, Sidney R., $300,000 loan. Late
payments for six months, I believe... Bartlett,
Robert T., $150,000, uncollectable... Ahh... this
one is interesting, Colson, Mrs. J. a $600,000
property, no payments since April and no
foreclosure proceedings...

FELLER
(indignant)
Her husband died. We're working out an
arrangement with her.

RAUSCH
I'm sure the Federal Home Loan Bank Board
will be very interested in your soft-heartedness.
(deadly serious)
You know what happens to Savings Banks that
have bad loans which exceed a certain
percentage of their assets... They can be forced
to merge into a larger and more solid institution.

FELLER
(interrupting vehemently)
Our percentages are fine!

RAUSCH
Oh no, they aren't... now! Haven't you
wondered about a recent upsurge in your loans
department? I must confess, we helped you a
bit... But, upon closer examination, you'll find
that some of those loans aren't worth the paper
they're printed on, as they say.

Feller has become red in the face. His confidence has
cracked. He sputters in indignation as he sits back down
in his chair.

FELLER
You... crook...

                         RAUSCH
        Tut... Tut... I believe you're also at the mercy of
        several recent, large depositors. If these people
        withdrew their funds, you would have to close.
        Some of them owe us favors, I just might want
        to collect on those...

Rausch stands up, walks to Feller's desk and slams his
hand down on it.

                         RAUSCH
        Enough of this bull. We have filed a petition
        with the Bank Board to take over your assets.
        The Federal Examiners have come to look at
        your books. They agree with our analysis...

Feller looks crushed. He has aged ten years in the last 15
minutes.

Rausch walks towards the door. Before he leaves, he
turns towards Feller.

                         RAUSCH
        Unlike what you said before, I don't like
        "unfriendly takeovers." They're usually messy,
        and not cost-effective... You have my number in
        L.A. Think it over, Feller.

He exits. Feller remains pensive for a moment. Then, he
gets up and walks out of his office.

INT. OCEAN SAVINGS - CORRIDOR - DAY
And from there to another office.

INT. OCEAN SAVINGS - BENNETT'S OFFICE - DAY
Bennett and Jesse are talking. Bennett is sitting behind his desk, and Jesse is standing next to him, showing him a loan application. They look up as Feller enters.

FELLER
(wiping his forehead)
Avery, something awful has happened. We have to talk.

Jesse picks up her papers.

JESSE
I'll come back later, Mr. Bennett.

She leaves, the two men hardly noticing her departure. She is careful not to close the door as she goes.

Feller sits down in a chair and starts to explain to Bennett.

FELLER
I just had a visit from Gordon Rausch, of Amalgamated Financial... They're after us. They want to build...

INT. OCEAN SAVINGS - CORRIDOR - DAY
Jesse stands near the door, shock written all over her face.

EXT. OCEAN SAVINGS - PARKING LOT - DAY
Jesse, wearing a light sweater, runs out of the front door, and towards her car.

She grabs open the door, throws her handbag into the back and jumps in. She looks flustered and upset.

The car burns rubber as it tears out of the lot.

EXT. SANTA BARBARA - DAY
Jesse driving at great speed through the traffic.

EXT. APARTMENT COMPLEX - DAY
The car pulls into its space at high speed and stops with a SCREECH. Jesse jumps out and runs up stairs into...

INT. APARTMENT - DAY
The apartment is neater than it used to be. There is more, new looking furniture. All in all, there is a more prosperous look about the place. Elliot sits at a new desk, compiling files for his book. Jesse suddenly bursts into the room.

DISSOLVE TO:

CLOSE-UP on two smoking coffee cups.

CAMERA PANS BACK to reveal Elliot and Jesse sitting at the kitchen table.

Elliot's face betrays his real concern, and certainly a feeling of responsibility that wasn't a part of his life in the past.

ELLIOT
We have to do something for them.

JESSE

I don't see what *we* could do. Amalgamated
Financial is such a powerful company. If what
Feller says is true, they've got Ocean at their
mercy.

ELLIOT

We can't just let them go under like that.
Besides, suppose they take a closer look at the
books. What would happen to us?

JESSE
(pensively)
That's right, I didn't think of that!... Feller asked
Bennett to call an emergency board meeting.
Perhaps they'll have a plan...

ELLIOT

Yeah, maybe. You know, I really like Feller.
He's pretty sharp. I bet he hasn't given up yet.

INT. OCEAN SAVINGS - BOARD ROOM - DAY
CLOSE-UP on Feller's face, grim and determined.

CAMERA PANS BACK to reveal the other Board
Members. Their faces mirror Feller's concern.

FELLER
...So, there you have it. As you can see, our
situation is critical. As I see it, we have two
options... give up or fight.

He looks at each Board Member in turn.

FELLER (cont'd)
I hope I am correct in assuming that you're all
behind me in this. I'm counting on you to help
me fight this dirty skunk, Rausch...

The Board Members nod their assent. Feller expresses
his satisfaction and gratitude.

FELLER (cont'd)
Thank you all. I'm glad to see that my hopes are
confirmed. I'll be honest with you, our chances
are small, very, very small.

He opens a folder that is lying on the table.

FELLER (cont'd)
Avery and I have prepared what we think is the
most workable strategy. We've spent a great
deal of time on the phone, with friends, business
associates, etc. It seems that this Rausch
character's hands are covered in dirt. Some of
our evidence is pretty damning...

He begins reviewing the documents.

FELLER (cont'd)
Kick-backs... Real estate deals where his friends
were the beneficiaries... Tax evasion, you name
it, he's done it.... Our plan is to present all the
evidence to the major shareholders of Amalgamated Financial. There is a general meeting
scheduled in three weeks. I'm sure most of them
are unaware of Rausch's shadier deals…

FELLER (cont'd)
Once we convince them, they'll kick him out
and we'll be safe.

Elliot has started to relax during the last part of Feller's speech. His fears are being allayed. The Chairman has a plan after all.

He starts lighting one of his expensive cigarettes, when Feller's next words catch him unprepared.

FELLER
(looking squarely at Elliot)
This is where we need your help, Royal.

ELLIOT
(almost dropping his cigarette)
Me! Yes, of course, but I don't see...

Feller becomes insistent.

FELLER
We want you to go to L.A. and speak to the
shareholders on our behalf. They'll be rich folks,
banks, insurance companies... You're
sophisticated, you have contacts. You speak
their language, not like the rest of us here.
They'll listen to you.

He fails to notice Elliot's stammering.

ELLIOT
But... but... but....

FELLER

Yes, I know it's a lot to ask... But, you see,
I fancy myself to be a good judge of people,
Royal. This morning, when I asked myself
whom I would trust to best act on our behalf, I
didn't have a moment's hesitation... In the past
few months, I feel we've gotten to know you
better, Royal. You may be a big city operator,
but at heart you're just like one of us. You're a
good, decent, honest man... I can't think of
anyone better equipped to go and tackle those
folks in L.A.

The other Board Members all nod in agreement.

KLEINMAN

Yeah, Royal. Sock it to 'em!

Elliot feels trapped. His integrity is really put to the test.
He could talk his way out of the job, yet his feelings tell
him he has no choice but to accept.

A PAUSE. Then:

ELLIOT

OK, Stan. I'll do it.

Feller jumps to his feet and goes to shake Elliot's hands.

FELLER

Oh, Royal, thank you! I knew we could count on
you!

The other Board Members get up, and in turn, they too thank Elliot.

>   KLEINMAN
>   If you need a backup, big fella, you can call on
>   me anytime.

>   GARDNER
>   Our firm will be pleased to give you any advice
>   you need. Here's my home phone number. Call
>   me anytime, day or night.

Elliot mutters thank yous.

>   ELLIOT
>   Thanks... I will... OK...

Then the Board Members leave.

Elliot starts to leave, too. As he passes Feller, he stops and looks at the Chairman.

ANOTHER PAUSE. For a minute Elliot wants to tell him everything.

>   ELLIOT
>   Stan, I...

>   FELLER
>   Yes, Royal?

But, he can't. It is not the fear of the law or of retribution that holds him back. He can't bear the idea of hurting his friend.

ELLIOT
...I'll do my best.

Feller puts his hand on Elliot's shoulder.

FELLER
I know, Royal. I know...

EXT. DOWNTOWN LOS ANGELES - DAY
AERIAL SHOT of Downtown L.A.

CAMERA ZOOMS IN on a medium-sized, old fash-
ioned, stone building, dwarfed by the neighboring glass
towers.

CLOSE-UP on a sign that reads: "HOTEL REGENCY."
CAMERA PANS TO a window.

INT. HOTEL ROOM - DAY
The room is a standard hotel one, clean, but a bit used.
Jesse is unpacking and putting clothes into a closet. We
SEE the "Royal Flush" outfit. Elliot sits on the bed, re-
viewing a notebook.

ELLIOT
So, it's agreed. You go to the library and dig up
the names and addresses of the major
shareholders, and I'll go to see them.

JESSE
What are you going to tell them?

Elliot pats the file which Feller gave him.

ELLIOT

I guess with all of this, it won't be that difficult.
Stan's done a lot of research. For instance, did
you know...

Jesse stops what she's doing and interrupts him. She's
been concerned all along, but expresses it for the first
time.

JESSE
(shaking her head)
I don't want to scare you, hon, but I wonder if
you've realized something. You've been able to
fool Feller and the others, but you're *not* Royal
Flush. The people that you have to convince
here are going to be a lot more sophisticated.
They may not fall for the act!

She comes and sits next to Elliot on the bed.

JESSE
(putting her hand on his shoulder)
Maybe we should just forget the whole thing...
Write to Feller. I can always find another job
somewhere else.

Elliot reacts vehemently. He now feels completely
committed to his role.

ELLIOT
We *can't* drop them like that! They're relying on
me! Rausch will eat them alive if we don't do
something about it!

                    JESSE
                 (discouraged)
        Rausch will eat *us* alive...

Elliot takes Jesse in his arms.

                    ELLIOT
                  (tenderly)
        Where's my superwoman now? Nothing
        bothered you before.

                    JESSE
        Before, I knew I could handle things. This is
        different...

                    ELLIOT
        Don't start worrying now. I can handle it. It'll be
        all right. Flush is like my other self.

                    JESSE
               (smiling ruefully)
        I thought it was "Catman?"

Elliot points his forefinger at the sky.

                    ELLIOT
        Us Dark Avengers of the Night all stick
        together!

EXT. L.A. LIBRARY - DAY
Jesse walks down 6th Street, turns left onto Hope Street
and sees...

JESSE'S POV - THE LOS ANGELES PUBLIC LI-
BRARY.

She walks up a flight of stairs and enters the Library.

INT. L.A. LIBRARY - DAY
Jesse sits at a table, surrounded by a number of large
volumes, directories, etc.

CLOSE-UP on her notepad, where she writes....

JESSE'S POV - "CALIFORNIA INSURANCE COM-
PANY"

MATCH CUT TO:

EXT. DOWNTOWN L.A. - ANOTHER LOCATION -
DAY
CLOSE-UP on a sign on a glass door that reads: "CALI-
FORNIA INSURANCE COMPANY."

CAMERA PANS BACK to reveal Elliot in his "Royal
Flush" attire, standing by the door, briefcase in hand.
After a second of hesitation, he opens the door and en-
ters.

INT. INSURANCE COMPANY - FORTY-THIRD
FLOOR LOBBY - DAY
An elevator door silently slides open. Elliot steps out
into a plush, elegantly furnished lobby. The floor is
lushly carpeted, the furniture is modern and tasteful, the
plants are a healthy green and the walls are decorated
with sedate, expensive paintings.

He orients himself, spots a receptionist's desk and walks towards it. The RECEPTIONIST raises her head and looks appreciatively at Elliot.

> ELLIOT
> I have an appointment with Mr. Brookes. My name is Roy...
> (a beat)
> ...Robert Flush. From Ocean Savings.

INT. INSURANCE COMPANY - BROOKES' OFFICE - DAY
CLOSE-UP on a plaque that reads - "WILLIAM D. BROOKES -PRESIDENT."

CAMERA PANS BACK to reveal a well-furnished office. The furniture is all in black and white, there are modern sculptures in the corners, the paintings are all abstract. The look is very high-tech. Two of the walls are full-size windows, giving a stunning view of Los Angeles.

Elliot sits in a designer chair. He has spread papers on the desk in front of him, behind which sits BROOKES, poker-faced. Brookes is a non-descript, "typical" businessman. He has a full head of thick, silvery hair, and appears to be in his late fifties.

He holds one of the documents in his hand while he reads it carefully. Then, he raises his eyes towards Elliot.

> BROOKES
> (giving himself time to think)
> Hmmm...

He gathers the documents, puts them into a neat stack and hands them back to Elliot.

                    BROOKES
          I'm afraid you've wasted your time, Mr. Flush.

Anticipating Elliot's objection, he raises his hand.

                    BROOKES (cont'd)
          Oh, I know. You've collected quite an
          impressive... um... file on Gordon Rausch. I can
          truly appreciate the concern of your board...

His face, however, reflects absolutely *no* feeling of concern. Brookes gets up and walks to a small table, grabs a cigar box, offers one to Elliot, who refuses, and takes one himself.

                    BROOKES
                 (closing the box)
          No? Too bad, they're real havanas.

He lights his cigar and takes a puff.

                    BROOKES
          You see, Mr. Flush. Even if what you say is
          true... and I'm not saying it is... this is of
          absolutely no concern to us. Insurance
          companies like ours are interested in one thing,
          and one thing only–the performance of the
          companies in which they own stock. I grant you
          that Amalgamated Financial and Gordie Rausch
          are a bit... mavericks of the financial
          community. But, their stock has regularly

BROOKES (cont'd)
outperformed the market. It appreciated 25%
in the last two years alone! That's what matters
to us. We must protect the value of our
investments. Frankly, we don't care if Gordie
Rausch goes out and mugs old ladies, as long as
his company's stock keeps climbing.

Elliot appears somewhat deflated.

ELLIOT
I see... I suppose you wouldn't at least consider
working to prevent a forced merger with Ocean
Savings?

BROOKES
(indifferent)
I don't think I could recommend such an action
to my board, no... Our interests in this matter are
the same as those of Amalgamated Financial.
Sorry, Mr. Flush.

Elliot realizes that there is nothing more that can be
done.

He gets up and perfunctorily shakes hands with Brookes.

ELLIOT
(slightly sarcastic)
Well, thank you for all your help.

BROOKES
(failing to notice the sarcasm)
Not at all. It's always a pleasure to be of service to a colleague.

Brookes watches as Elliot leaves the room. He remains pensive for a few seconds, then goes to his desk and pushes a button on the intercom.

BROOKES
Katy, get me Gordie Rausch on the phone...

EXT. BEVERLY HILLS - DAY
ESTABLISHING SHOT of a glass tower.

CLOSE-UP on a sign that reads - "AMALGAMATED FINANCIAL–WE BUILD A BETTER TOMORROW TODAY."

INT. RAUSCH'S OFFICE - DAY
This is another modern, well-decorated office. However, it looks less personal and more as if actual work takes place here. Rausch is working behind a large, glass desk. His telephone RINGS.

SECRETARY (V.O)
Mr. Brookes is on line two, Mr. Rausch.

RAUSCH
I'll take him.
(pushing one of the phone's buttons)
Hello, Willy. What's cooking in the insurance business?

He listens to a long explanation, punctuating his silence only by an occasional nod and a grunted, "uh huh." The explanation finally reaches its end.

                    RAUSCH
          I see... Thanks for the warning...
                    (a beat)
          Yes... of course I intend to do something about
          it... No, don't worry... Thanks again, Willy...
          Yes... I'll see you on the 15th. Bye.

He hangs up. His face then assumes an expression of rage.

                    RAUSCH
          Those bastards. I'll show them...
                    (pressing on the intercom)
          Send Joe in right away.

INT. OUTSIDE RAUSCH'S OFFICE - CORRIDOR - DAY
We HEAR "Jaws"-like MUSIC as we follow Joe from behind, walking down the corridor to...

INT. RAUSCH'S OFFICE - DAY
Joe enters the office.

                    JOE
          You wanted me, Mr. Rausch?

Rausch looks coldly at his henchman and cracks his knuckles.

                    RAUSCH
          Yes, Joe. A man named Robert Flush has been
          calling on some of our associates. I want to
          know who he is, where he comes from, what he
          wants... everything.

Joe looks as if he hasn't quite understood what Rausch
wants.

                    JOE
          Do ya want me to rough him up a little bit?

Rausch's face creases into a cold smile.

                    RAUSCH
          No. Not...
                    (a beat)
          ...yet. Now, go.

Joe turns and leaves the room.

Rausch cracks his knuckles once or twice more. He
starts fingering through a box of business cards, and
pulls several of them out. He then grabs the telephone
and starts dialing.

                    RAUSCH
          Martha McClure, please... Yes, J. Gordon
          Rausch...
                    (a beat)
          Hello, Martha... Fine, and you... I wanted to let
          you know that someone by the name of Robert
          Flush might be calling on you...

                        102

EXT. LOS ANGELES - ANOTHER LOCATION - DAY
Elliot looks at one of the index cards prepared by Jesse, then at

ELLIOT'S POV - A GLASS OFFICE BUILDING
He enters.

INT. A PLUSH OFFICE - DAY
Elliot shakes hands with a middle-aged BUSINESS MAN. Their conversation is at an end. Elliot appears to be discouraged.

ELLIOT
Well, thank you for your time, anyway.

A SERIES OF QUICK CUTS BETWEEN THE LIBRARY AND ELLIOT'S UNSUCCESSFUL CALLS.

INT. L.A. LIBRARY - DAY
Jesse is filling out more index cards.

INT. ANOTHER OFFICE - DAY
Elliot is presenting his documents to a group of three EXECUTIVES. He appears to be trying very hard to break their indifference.

INT. L.A. LIBRARY - DAY
Jesse working.

INT. YET ANOTHER OFFICE - DAY
Elliot walks out the door and slowly closes it behind him. His face is even more dejected.

INT. L.A. LIBRARY - DAY
Jesse working.

EXT. BEVERLY HILLS STREET - DAY
Elliot is driving a rented car, looking back and forth
between the street addresses and one of Jesse's index
cards.

                    ELLIOT
          Let's see... 450 North Cañon...

INT. BANK PRESIDENT'S OFFICE - DAY
Elliot listens to a sympathetic-looking BANK PRESI-
DENT.

                    PRESIDENT
          I'll take what you've told me into consideration,
          Mr. Flush. But, frankly, I wouldn't be too
          hopeful if I were you... Confidentially, I'm not
          too crazy about Gordon Rausch myself. What
          you've shown me just confirms my own
          feelings. If you manage to get a substantial
          opposition going, I'll be happy to throw my
          support behind you. But, otherwise, my hands
          are tied. I'm sure you understand...

                    ELLIOT
               (sighing)
          Well, I guess that's something. Thanks for the
          kind words, anyway. Maybe things will work
          out after all...

                    PRESIDENT
          Yes, stay in touch. Let me know what happens.

The two men shake hands.

EXT. REGENCY HOTEL - NIGHT
ESTABLISHING SHOT of the hotel.

INT. HOTEL ROOM - NIGHT
Jesse sits at the table. She is filling in more index cards.
Elliot enters.

                    ELLIOT
               (tired)
          Hi, hon.

                    JESSE
               (anxious)
          How did it go today?

Elliot crumples on the bed.

                    ELLIOT
          Not good. They're not interested. Thanks, but no
          thanks. Some of these guys couldn't care less if
          Rausch had killed his own mother... Once in a
          while, somebody's a bit more receptive, but

                    ELLIOT (cont'd)
          I don't think we'll be able to do much unless we
          get more people on our side.

Jesse comes and puts a hand on his shoulder, then she
points at the files.

                    JESSE
          Well, don't get discouraged. There are still a
          bunch of names we haven't contacted yet.

CLOSE-UP on Elliot's face showing definite signs of
tiredness and discouragement.

<u>EXT. WILSHIRE BOULEVARD - DAY</u>
Elliot parks his car in front of a building. He gets out and
walks into a lobby.

<u>INT. LOBBY - DAY</u>
Elliot approaches a receptionist.

                    ELLIOT
          I'm here to see Miss McClure.

                    RECEPTIONIST
               (coolly)
          Sorry, but Miss McClure had to cancel her
          appointment.

Elliot feels upset, but remains outwardly calm.

                    ELLIOT
          But, it's the third time this week...

                    RECEPTIONIST
               (filing her nails)
          Well, I'm sorry, but there's nothing *I* can do
          about it.

Elliot disgusted, walks out in rage.

EXT. WILSHIRE BOULEVARD - DAY
Elliot storms out of the building walking back towards his car.

As he prepares to get in, he is FRAMED in the view-finder of a camera's telephoto lens. We HEAR the WHIRRING NOISE of several photos being taken.

CAMERA TURNS 180 DEGREES to reveal Joe taking the pictures.

He then jumps into the car, brutally inserts himself into traffic and starts to follow Elliot.

EXT. LOS ANGELES FREEWAY - DAY
VARIOUS ANGLES of the two cars following each other.

INT. ELLIOT'S CAR - DAY
CLOSE-UP on Elliot, unaware that he is being followed.

EXT. DOWNTOWN GARAGE - DAY
Elliot's car pulls into the garage. Joe's car follows right behind.

EXT. REGENCY HOTEL - DUSK
Elliot walks into the hotel.

CAMERA PANS BACK to reveal Joe on the other side of the street.

INT. HOTEL ROOM - DUSK
Elliot is lying on the bed, looking very depressed.

Jesse is sitting next to him, trying to comfort him, but she too looks gloomy.

                        ELLIOT
            There sure are a lot of sharks out there...
            What's the point, honey? The truth is, that
            nobody cares. Nobody cares about what will
            happen to Ocean Savings. Nobody cares about
            Rausch being a crook. Nobody cares about the
            people who will lose their homes. Nobody cares
            about anything except their damn stock!

                        JESSE
            Maybe some of them will change their minds.
            You said yourself...

                        ELLIOT
            That will be the day! No they won't!... You
            know, I wonder if Rausch isn't on to us... I've
            had the feeling that some of those people have
            been warned about me.

                        JESSE
            Don't go getting paranoid about all this. Even if
            it's true, there's nothing he can do about it.

                        ELLIOT
                    (frowning)
            I don't know. I just think it's suspicious.

                        JESSE
            Why don't you call Cliff? That'll cheer you up.

ELLIOT

That's a good idea.

Elliot crawls to the end of the bed and grabs the telephone. He dials Cliff's number.

ELLIOT

Hi, pal, it's me... No, not too good up till now...
Boy, you should see some of these people.
They'd make "Uncle Scrooge" look like "Little
Lulu!"... Yeah, otherwise it's nice. It's full of
weird looking people here...

EXT. REGENCY HOTEL - ACROSS THE STREET - NIGHT

Joe crushes a cigarette under his heel, then leaves.
CLOSE-UP on the cigarette butt.

DISSOLVE TO:

EXT. REGENCY HOTEL - DAY

CLOSE-UP on the same butt being washed away by the
street cleaning machine. It is a bright and fresh new
morning.

CAMERA PANS TO Elliot and Jesse coming out of the
hotel. Elliot kisses her.

ELLIOT

OK, hon. Have a good day. See ya later,
alligator!

We HEAR the WHIRRING SOUND of photos being
taken.

CAMERA PANS QUICKLY to the right to focus on Joe who then crosses the street and walks into...

INT. REGENCY HOTEL LOBBY - DAY
Joe walks to the reception desk. A CLERK comes out from an adjacent office, looking bored.

                    CLERK
          Yeah?

Joe puts a 50 dollar bill on the counter. The clerk suddenly looks less bored.

                    JOE
          I wanna talk to ya, kid...

EXT. ROYAL FLUSH COMICS - DAY
ESTABLISHING SHOT of the shop. A car comes into view, then slides to a standstill.

CAMERA ZOOMS IN on the driver. It is Joe. He starts taking photos with a camera and a telephoto lens.

EXT. WAREHOUSE - DAY
Cliff is washing his car in the driveway.

CAMERA PANS BACK to reveal Joe taking more pictures.

INT. SANTA BARBARA - A COFFEE SHOP - DAY
Joe sits at a table with a young blonde GIRL that looks, and sounds bubble-headed. She wears a badge that identifies her as an employee of Ocean Savings.

GIRL
...and I said to her, Ellen, you've taken two
hours for lunch and I've been here since...

Joe pulls a picture of Jesse out of his wallet. We SEE
that it is the picture taken in front of the hotel.

JOE
(pointing at Jesse's picture)
Do you know this girl? What's her name?

The Girl looks at the picture closely.

GIRL
That's Jesse Lawrence. She works with
Mr. Bennett in Operations. Who's that guy with
her, her boy friend? He's really cute...

CLOSE-UP on the photo.

MATCH CUT TO:

INT. RAUSCH'S HOUSE - NIGHT
CLOSE-UP on the same photo.

CAMERA PANS BACK to reveal a beautifully furnished living room. In a corner is a fireplace with tro-
phies and awards on it. On the walls are expensive litho-
graphs. Rausch sits on a leather couch. In front of him,
on a coffee table, are all the photos taken by Joe.

RAUSCH
This is amazing, Joe. Beautiful work.

Joe stands in the middle of the room. A smile slowly crosses his face.

                            JOE
Thank you, Mr. Rausch.

                          RAUSCH
                      (with an evil grin)
Tomorrow, I'll make that sucker Feller cry. You hear me, cry...

Rausch goes to a big window, through which we can see Los Angeles at night. CAMERA ZOOMS IN on the downtown area.

INT. HOTEL ROOM - NIGHT
Elliot is in his pajamas, brushing his teeth in the bathroom. As he rinses out the toothpaste, he shouts to Jesse.

                          ELLIOT
          That shareholders' meeting is in a couple of
          days, and we've barely lined up any support. I
          don't have any idea what we're going to do.

Jesse is making piles of file cards on the bed.

                          JESSE
                        (frowning)
          There may still be a chance, you know.

Elliot puts his head around the edge of the bathroom door.

ELLIOT

What do you mean, a chance? I feel like I've
talked to everybody in this damn city!

Jesse grabs a small stack of index cards.

JESSE

You see all of these files... Ghost Limited...
Magic Investments... The Chance Money Fund...
It seems that all these companies belong to the
same man. He's a private investor who made his
fortune in patents or something, after the World
War II. Together, they own about 31% of Amalgamated Financial. If we could get hold of this
guy, we could get the leverage we need. But, I
haven't been able to find his address yet...

Elliot steps into the room. He appears intrigued.

ELLIOT

You know, that's funny...

JESSE

What?

ELLIOT

Those names... Ghost, Magic, Chance...

JESSE
(uncomprehendingly)
What's wrong with them?

ELLIOT

They're all obscure comic book characters...

ELLIOT (cont'd)
...From before the War. "The Ghost," "Mister Magic," "Miss Chance"... All uncredited of course...

JESSE
(smiling)
Maybe the guy is a comic book fan, like you. That would be great.

ELLIOT
What's his name?

Jesse looks among her files.

JESSE
Rensie. William Rensie.

Elliot smacks his head with the flat of his hand.

ELLIOT
Will Rensie! That's it! I can't believe it!

JESSE
What? What is it?

ELLIOT
Rensie was a famous ghost artist before the War. He drew the sexiest girls of all time! That was his trademark. Nobody knows much about him except for a few experts. He must have drawn all these characters! What a find for my book!

A beat.

ELLIOT (cont'd)

He hasn't done anything since. He just
disappeared. He always was a real secretive kind
of guy...

JESSE

Well, that doesn't seem to have changed any. I
can't find him anywhere.

ELLIOT
(agitated)

But you've *got* to find him! He's our last
chance! I know him... I mean, I know the stories
he used to draw. He'll listen to me. If I can talk
to him, we're saved!

INT. RAUSCH'S OFFICE - DAY

Rausch, a vicious expression on his face, starts dialing
the telephone.

RAUSCH
(to himself)

...cry...
(a beat)

Yes... Mr. Feller... Yes, J. Gordon Rausch... Yes,
it's important...
(another beat)

RAUSCH (cont'd)

Hello, Feller! Rausch here. I've got some news
that I thought might be of interest to you. It
concerns your associate, Mr. Robert Flush... or
should I say, Mr. Elliot Martin...

INT. OCEAN SAVINGS - FELLER'S OFFICE - DAY
CLOSE-UP on Feller's face, as his eyes widen and he starts registering the shock of what he has just heard.

INT. RAUSCH'S OFFICE – DAY

                    RAUSCH
                (enjoying himself)
        ...Don't take my word for it. Do your own
        checking, if you wish. I'll call you back in an
        hour. In light of all this, I hope you'll begin to
        see things my way.

He hangs up.

INT. OCEAN SAVINGS - FELLER'S OFFICE - DAY
Feller is still holding the telephone. He finally puts it down, looking as if he is still suffering from the shock of the news.

He walks out of the office like a zombie.

INT. OCEAN SAVINGS - BENNETT'S OFFICE - DAY
Bennett is behind his desk, working. Feller enters, still looking very pale.

                    FELLER
        Avery, what happened to your assistant, you
        know, that pretty blonde girl?

                    BENNETT
        Jessica? She took a couple of weeks vacation.
        Why?

He notices Feller's rather emotional state.

>BENNETT
>Is anything wrong, Stan? You look like you've
>seen a ghost.

>FELLER
>(with a weak smile)
>I wish I had, Avery, I wish I had.
>(a beat)
>Give me the file on Royal Flush, please...

Bennett goes to a drawer and pulls out the file. He hands
it to Feller, his face registering his worry.

>BENNETT
>Something is wrong, Stan. I can feel it. Why
>don't you tell me about it?

>FELLER
>(walking out of the room)
>I can't, Avery. Not yet.

INT. OCEAN SAVINGS - FELLER'S OFFICE - DAY
Feller is sitting at his desk, his face buried in his hands.

CLOSE-UP on the file and the forms that he has spread
in front of him.

CAMERA PANS TO the telephone that RINGS.

Feller looks at it suspiciously. Then, his face adopts an
expression of firm resolution. It is like that of the "old"

Feller, but with a harder edge to it. He has been hurt, but he has overcome it.

                         FELLER
          Hello?... Yes. I do have an answer for you, Mr.
          Rausch... The same answer. No.

CAMERA ZOOMS IN on Feller's face to highlight his growing determination.

                         FELLER
          In spite of your accusations, and of what Mr.
          Flush... or Martin... may or may not have done, I
          retain all of my confidence in him. Since the
          beginning of our relationship, Mr... yes... Mr.
          Flush has shown himself to be, in all aspects, a
          wise and dependable individual... No, don't
          interrupt me, please. We have entrusted him
          with a mission, and I'm sure he'll carry it out to
          the best of his abilities... That's all. Good-bye,
          Mr. Rausch.

He hangs up, and then looks pensively into space.

<u>INT. RAUSCH'S OFFICE - DAY</u>
Rausch's face contorts in rage as he slams the telephone receiver down, and then sends the instrument crashing to the floor.

                         RAUSCH
          That bastard! I'll show him! Nobody does that to
          J. Gordon Rausch...
                    (shouting)
          Joe! Joe!

Joe rushes into the office.

JOE

Is something wrong, Mr. Rausch?

RAUSCH

Get rid of him, Joe! Trash him, break him, do what you want with him, but I don't want to hear about that son of a bitch Flush ever again!

JOE

(smiling)
Yes sir, Mr. Rausch!

EXT. DOWNTOWN GARAGE - DAY
Elliot's car pulls into the lot.

INT. DOWNTOWN GARAGE - DAY
Elliot locks the door of his car.

JOE (O.S.)

Hey, Martin!

Elliot turns, surprised and sees Joe and two THUGS coming out of a parked van. Elliot backs up, scared.

ELLIOT

Who are you? What do you want?

JOE

The game is over, "Flush." We know everything! Your girl friend, the $250,000, the comic book shop... My boss spoke to Feller, you're all washed up!

119

ELLIOT
(dumbstruck)
Your boss?

JOE
Mr. Rausch!

Elliot starts to run. The two thugs easily catch up with him, grab him and drag him back into the van.

Joe checks for witnesses, cracks his knuckles, jumps into the back of the van and closes the door.

We HEAR muffled sounds of BLOWS and CRIES.

DISSOLVE TO:

CLOSE-UP on Elliot's face, swollen, bruised and bleeding. His eyes are closed.

JANITOR (O.S.)
Mister! Hey, mister!

Elliot opens one eye.

CAMERA PANS BACK to show him lying on the floor, not far from his car. The van is gone. A JANITOR is shaking him gently.

JANITOR
Mister, are you OK?

Elliot props himself up painfully.

ELLIOT
Ugh! I hurt all over!
(a beat)
Oh my God, Jesse!...
(to the janitor)
Thanks a lot. I'll be OK... I've got to get out of
here!

He runs away, limping.

INT. REGENCY HOTEL LOBBY - NIGHT
Elliot crosses the lobby and rushes into an elevator.

INT. HOTEL ROOM - NIGHT
Elliot bursts into the room. It is in a shambles, their
clothes have been shredded, the stack of files is gone. He
sits on the bed, totally drained of energy and puts his
head in his hands.

A LONG PAUSE.

Jesse walks in.

JESSE
Honey? Guess what I...

She takes in the disaster in one glance and rushes to
Elliot.

JESSE
Oh my God! Elliot, what happened?

ELLIOT
(defeated)
We're finished, hon. Rausch has found out...
about everything. He sent some of his...
"employees" after me...

Jesse checks Elliot's cuts and bruises to make sure he
isn't seriously hurt.

JESSE
Oh, Elliot. My poor Elliot. Are you hurt?

ELLIOT
I don't think so. Not seriously, anyway. I think
it's going to be a while before I can walk
straight though... But, things are even worse.
One of them told me that Rausch talked to
Feller...

The gravity of Elliot's statement suddenly sinks in.

JESSE
Oh no!

ELLIOT
Yeah. Not only are we finished, we'll be lucky if
we don't go to jail. We were a little like children
playing on the freeway. We've just been run
over by a truck.
(a beat)
I guess there aren't really any Dark Avengers.

JESSE
What are we going to do?

ELLIOT
I don't know... I just don't know.

Jesse and Elliot sit on the bed, holding each other tight. They feel that they have really reached bottom. They have nowhere to go, and there is no one that they can turn to for help. Their whole world has crumbled around them.

There is a LONG SILENCE. Somewhere, we hear a clock TICKING.

Suddenly, the telephone RINGS. Jesse picks it up without thinking. Then, she almost drops it.

JESSE
It's Feller! What do we do?

ELLIOT
Let me talk to him. I owe the man that much...

Elliot reaches out his hand and takes the receiver.

ELLIOT
Hello, Mr. Feller. I don't know what to say...

INT. OCEAN SAVINGS - FELLER' OFFICE - NIGHT
Feller sits at his desk, a look of apprehension on his face.

FELLER
Then, don't say anything, my dear Royal.
I called to see how you... and your lovely friend
Jessica... were doing.

His voice is falsely jolly, as if nothing had happened, but you can hear the underlying tension.

INT. HOTEL ROOM - NIGHT
The reference to Jesse does not escape Elliot's notice.

> ELLIOT
> (almost speechless)
> Jessica...

INT. OCEAN SAVINGS - FELLER'S OFFICE - NIGHT

> FELLER
> Yes, Jessica... My son once had a girl friend named Jessica... Did I ever tell about my son, Royal? I guess not. He was a bit of a rogue. He used to do things that weren't... well, not exactly illegal, but not very honest either. Sometimes the law would catch up with him, and other times it wouldn't... But, people always gave him a second chance. Do you know why, Royal?

INT. HOTEL ROOM - NIGHT

> ELLIOT
> (shaking his head)
> No.

INT. OCEAN SAVINGS - FELLER'S OFFICE - NIGHT

FELLER
Because at heart, he was basically a good and
decent person. His friends knew it. That's why
they always gave him another chance.... If my
son had *really* been dishonest, well, I expect he
would have just skipped town and vanished. He
wouldn't have stayed with his family and
friends. Don't you agree, Royal?

INT. HOTEL ROOM - NIGHT
There is a LONG SILENCE, while the meaning of Feller's speech sinks in.

ELLIOT
(firmer)
Yes, I agree, Stan... He would have stayed and
helped his friends.

INT. OCEAN SAVINGS - FELLER'S OFFICE -
NIGHT
Feller sighs in relief and happiness. His judgment of
Elliot's character has been confirmed.

FELLER
I knew you'd say that, Royal.
(a beat)
But, I've been rambling on and I forgot to
mention the real reason for this call. That
shareholders' meeting is tomorrow, and I wanted
to wish you luck, Royal. Really give it to them!
We're all counting on you. We know you'll do
your best...
(a hint of doubt creeps into his voice)
...won't you?

INT. HOTEL ROOM – NIGHT

                    ELLIOT
                (firm)
        Of course, Stan. I will...
                (a beat)
        ... And Jesse will, too.

                    FELLER (V.O.)
        Fine, fine... I knew you would. Well, I guess
        that's all. Good night.

                    ELLIOT
        Good night to you too, Stan... and, God Bless
        you.

We HEAR the SOUND OF THE PHONE being hung up
at the other end.

Elliot hangs up the receiver. He has a faraway look on
his face, as if he still doesn't quite believe what has happened.

Jesse has been trying to listen to the conversation, and
although she got most of it, she's avid for details.

                    JESSE
        What happened? What did he say?

Elliot answers as if he hasn't heard the question. His
eyes are still looking elsewhere.

ELLIOT

I think... we've been granted a reprieve.

JESSE
(incredulous)
What!

ELLIOT

He told me a story about his son...

JESSE

(frowning)
His son? I didn't know he had one. I don't even
think he's ever been married.

ELLIOT

I don't think that was the point of the story...
(turning towards Jesse, with energy)
We have to do anything we can to save him.
Have you found Rensie's address yet?

Jesse becomes excited again.

JESSE

Yes, that's what I was going to tell you when
I came in. I found it! He lives in a big, secluded
estate in Bel Air...

Elliot gets up, slams his fist into the palm of his other
hand.

ELLIOT
(with excitement)
Great! Then here's what we'll do. Tomorrow,
you'll go to the meeting, and I'll try to see
Rensie. You take a copy of the documents with
you, and stall things for as long as you can.
Meanwhile, I'll talk to him... We can't blow it.
This is our last chance...

EXT. DOWNTOWN GARAGE - DAY
Elliot's car zooms out of the building and into the traffic.

EXT. DOWNTOWN LOS ANGELES - DAY
Jesse walks along the street. She is dressed in a stylish
business suit and carries a briefcase in hand. She looks
up at...

JESSE'S POV - THE BONAVENTURE HOTEL.
On the marquee, a SIGN reads: "WELCOME AMAL-
GAMATED FINANCIAL SHAREHOLDERS."

Jesse nods to herself, and walks into the hotel.

EXT. BEL AIR - DAY
Elliot's car drives off Sunset Blvd. into one of Bel Air's
streets. The car slows down, as Elliot starts looking for
the address.

INT. BONAVENTURE HOTEL - DAY
CLOSE-UP on a sign board that lists the location of the
various meetings taking place in the hotel.

CAMERA ZOOMS IN on one such listing that reads: "AMALGAMATED FINANCIAL - ESMERALDA ROOM."

CAMERA PANS BACK to reveal Jesse, orienting herself. Jesse then proceeds to the Esmeralda Room, where TWO GIRLS sit at a table, taking down names and giving out badges, and envelopes containing the meeting agenda and various bits of information. ANOTHER GIRL stands next to a coffee urn, and offers cups to the arrivals.

Jesse walks to the table and gets registered.

EXT. BEL AIR - DAY
Elliot looks like he has found the address. It is...

ELLIOT'S POV - A huge mansion partially hidden by vegetation. The entrance is closed off by an impressive looking gate, behind which a liveried guard patrols.

Elliot whistles to himself in admiration.

INT. BONAVENTURE - ESMERALDA ROOM - DAY
Jesse walks into the room with circumspection. It is a large room with rows of chairs, which start filling up as more people walk in. At one end is a dais, upon which sits Amalgamated Financial's management.

CAMERA ZOOMS IN on Rausch, exchanging words with the Treasurer of the Company, who sits next to him. Jesse takes a chair in the second row and sits down.

EXT. RENSIE'S MANSION - DAY

Elliot strolls down to the gate. He tries to hide his anxiety, but we can SEE that he knows this is his last chance, and he is concerned.

Elliot grabs hold of the gate and waves to attract the attention of the GUARD.

> ### ELLIOT
> Hey, Mister!

The Guard swaggers towards him.

> ### GUARD
> Yeah... what is it?

> ### ELLIOT
> I've got to see Mr. Rensie, it's really important!

> ### GUARD
> Mr. Rensie don't see no one!

Elliot grows more agitated and starts shaking the bars.

> ### ELLIOT
> He's got to see me! You have to let me see him! It's a matter of life and death!

The Guard completely ignores Elliot's appeal.

INT. BONAVENTURE - ESMERALDA ROOM - DAY

The meeting is in progress. CAMERA PANS over the faces in the audience. We recognize several of the people visited by Elliot. Joe stands discreetly to the far side of the dais.

THE TREASURER is concluding his speech. Jesse shifts nervously in her seat. Rausch thanks the Treasurer.

                    RAUSCH
          Thank you, Arthur.... You have heard our report.
          It has been an excellent year for your company.
          And now, it is the time when we open the floor
          to you, the shareholders, the true owners of this
          company, to ask your questions. This will be
          followed by the traditional vote of confidence in
          your management.

Jesse raises her hand and stands up.

                    RAUSCH
          Yes... The pretty lady in the second row...

                    JESSE
          I have a question... In fact, I have several
          questions...

She starts referring to the documents that she holds in her hands.

                    JESSE (cont'd)
          First, I want to draw the attention of this meeting
          to the unconscionable business practices of
          Mr. Rausch's management. I am referring to, in
          particular...

Rausch signals to Joe while Jesse speaks. Joe obediently approaches his boss.

> RAUSCH
> (whispering, teeth clenched)
> Who is she?

> JOE
> I think she's that guy's girl friend.

> RAUSCH
> (seething)
> I thought you had taken care of them.

> JOE
> You want me to get rid of her?

A PAUSE.

> RAUSCH
> No. Not yet... Besides, I don't think she can really hurt us. The majority is still with us.

EXT. RENSIE'S MANSION - DAY
The Guard is still standing at the gate, now looking annoyed and threatening.

> GUARD
> I don't know what your game is, Mister, but if you don't cut it out, I'm going to have to call the cops...

Elliot is on his knees, clinging to the gate with both hands.

ELLIOT
(begging)
Please, please, let me talk to him. I know he'll want to see me... At least *check with him*! If he says no, I promise I'll go away.

The Guard thinks for a minute, and decides that it's worth it to get rid of Elliot. He walks to an intercom which is located on his side of the gate, and dials.

GUARD
(respectfully)
Mr. Rensie? I'm sorry to bother you, I have a guy here that...

Elliot puts his head to the bars and shouts.

ELLIOT
Mr. Rensie, I know you drew "The Ghost" and "Mister Magic" and "Miss Chance" too!

A LONG PAUSE.

GUARD
(baffled)
Yes...
(turning to look at Elliot)
Well, I'd say he's about 30, and he's wearing a white suit...

Elliot begins to feel that victory will be his.

ELLIOT
(shouting)
Nobody has ever drawn girls as gorgeous as
yours!

ANOTHER LONG PAUSE.

GUARD
(subdued)
Yes, sir... Yes, of course, Mr. Rensie... I'll let
him in now, sir.

The Guard turns grudgingly towards the gate, and opens
it. Elliot walks haughtily past him and towards the house
to the tune of "Catman."

INT. BONAVENTURE - ESMERALDA ROOM - DAY
Jesse looks tired, slightly disheveled and flushed. She
has obviously been speaking for a while.

Rausch looks like he's had enough. With barely con-
tained rage, he interrupts her in the middle of a sentence
by BANGING the gavel on the dais.

RAUSCH
This meeting has had enough of your antics,
Miss Lawrence. It's time to take the vote.

JESSE
(shouting)
You won't silence me, like you did the others!
You're a crook, and everybody in this room
knows it!

134

She turns towards the shareholders.

> JESSE (cont'd)
> (beseeching)
> Yesterday, this man sent his goons to beat up my boy friend... Listen to me! You've heard what Rausch has done. You've heard what he's planning to do! How can you entrust your money to someone like him? Even if I fail to convince you today, sooner or later he's going to go too far and you'll all be dragged down with him! I appeal to you to...

SOME OF THE SHAREHOLDERS fidget in their chairs, their faces showing doubt and second thoughts.

Rausch again BANGS his gavel and signals to Joe.

> RAUSCH
> (shouting)
> I'll have you expelled from this meeting!

Joe walks towards Jesse, menacingly. Jesse moves away from him, while still haranguing the audience.

Joe catches up with her, picks her up and starts to drag her from the room.

Jesse claws at him, and almost manages to free herself, while screaming.

> JESSE
> Unhand me, you big...

But in vain. She is effectively silenced.

SOME OF THE SHAREHOLDERS look increasingly uncomfortable. A few start to BOO.

CAMERA PANS TO several JOURNALISTS, scratching avidly in their notebooks.

Rausch tries to calm the audience.

>   RAUSCH
>   (coolly)
>   I apologize for this regrettable incident. This
>   young woman is obviously disturbed... We shall
>   now proceed to take the vote... Following
>   general procedure, the secretary will call each
>   shareholder to stand up and cast their votes for
>   or against management.

CAMERA PANS TO the right of the dais.

The Company's SECRETARY starts calling names in alphabetical order.

>   SECRETARY
>   Anderson, Sydney J., voting on behalf of the
>   Mutual Fund of Nebraska, 0.30% of the shares...

ANDERSON stands. He looks hesitant, casts a glance at Jesse, then votes.

>   ANDERSON
>   (guiltily)
>   For.

He sits down, and looks again at Jesse.

> SECRETARY (O.S.)
> Angeletti, Arthur O., voting for himself. 0.12%
> of the shares...

> ANGELETTI
> (standing up)
> Against.

Rausch looks upset and frowns.

THE VOTING CONTINUES

A number of people vote against Rausch, including
some that Elliot had spoken to.

> SECRETARY
> Palk, Leslie R., voting for First Pacific Bank,
> 9.5% of the shares...

PALK stands up. We recognize the bank president that
was sympathetic to Elliot.

> PALK
> (firmly)
> Against.

Rausch worried, turns to the Treasurer, who has been
keeping his own tab, and leans towards him.

                    RAUSCH
                  (sotto vocce)
            Where do we stand now?

The Treasurer enters some figures into a calculator.

                    TREASURER
                    (ditto)
            Well, let's see... We own 30% of our own
            stock... Now, with the people that have voted
            for us, that gives us... let's see 43%...
                  (turning towards Rausch)
            We're a bit short. She's managed to turn a lot of
            people against you, but the voting isn't over yet.
            We still stand a good chance of coming out
            ahead. Especially, if some of the shareholders
            don't show up... and lots of them never do.

                  SECRETARY (O.S.)
            Roland, David E., voting for Mayfield
            Insurance, 4.2% of the shares...

                    WALLACE (O.S.)
            For.

                    TREASURER
            Well, with him, that gives us slightly over 47%.
            I think you're in.

Rausch smiles, reassured. His eyes narrow down as he
looks at Jesse, still being held by Joe.

SECRETARY
Rensie, William, voting for Ghost Limited,
Magic Investments and The Chance Money
Fund... 30.7% of the shares...

ELLIOT (O.S.)
Against!

CLOSE-UP on Jesse's face, lighting up in relief.

CLOSE-UP on Rausch's face, registering a mix of surprise and fear.

Jesse manages to push a surprised Joe back.

JESSE
Elliot!

CAMERA PANS TO Elliot, who has just walked into the room.

Elliot exhibits a huge grin as he brandishes a piece of paper.

ELLIOT
I hold all the proxies for Mr. Rensie's shares,
and I vote to get rid of Rausch!

CAMERA ZOOMS IN on Rausch, looking pale and utterly defeated.

Joe releases Jesse, who runs towards Elliot.

The Shareholders APPLAUD.

EXT. ROYAL FLUSH COMICS - DAY
ESTABLISHING SHOT of the shop, which looks sparkling under a fresh coat of paint and a new sign.

INT. ROYAL FLUSH COMICS - DAY
There is an atmosphere of exuberance in the shop. Elliot and Jesse are very excited as they talk to Cliff, who sits behind the counter, looking extremely happy.

                    ELLIOT
          ...and guess what? Mr. Rensie said that he would
          come down for an autograph party!

                    CLIFF
          Oh, wow!

                    JESSE
          And that's not all! This morning, Mr. Feller told
          Elliot that he had fixed everything so the money
          really belongs to us now. He wants Elliot to run
          for Board Chairman when he retires next year!

                    CLIFF
          What are you going to do with all of the money,
          now that it's not a secret?

Jesse links her arm through Elliot's.

                    JESSE
          Well, we're going to buy ourselves a ranch...

                    ELLIOT
          Yeah, we'll call it "Dark Avenger's Retreat!"

They all laugh. CAMERA PANS BACK AND OUT of
the shop as we...

FADE OUT.

THE END

ABOUT THE AUTHORS

Writers **Jean-Marc & Randy LOFFICIER** have co-authored five screenplays, a dozen books and numerous comic books and translations. They have collaborated on a number of animation teleplays, including episodes of *Duck Tales* and *The Real Ghostbusters* and written such popular characters as *Superman* and *Doctor Strange*. In 1999, in recognition of their distinguished career as comic book writers, editors and translators, they were presented with the Inkpot award for Outstanding Achievement in Comic Arts. Randy is a member of the Writers Guild of America, West and Mystery Writers of America.